dance in the rain

dina ezzeddine

CONTENTS

DEDICATION

Thanks to everyone who made my first poetry book a success "**coffee season**" was #1 for a long time in all platforms. Thank you so much!

This book is dedicated to the beautiful country of Japan, the country I love. Its elegance and beauty is unmatched in this world.

INTRODUCTION
Welcome Readers

Welcome readers to the world of Japanese Haiku and poems. What is a Haiku? A Haiku is a Japanese poem that consists of three lines, with five syllables in the first line, seven in the second line and five in the third line. Haiku is developed from the hokku, the opening three lines of a longer poem known as a tanka. The Haiku became a separate form of poetry in the 17th century.

The full term of the work haiku is derived from the first element of the word *haikai* (a humorous form of *renga,* or linked verse poem).

This book will also contain free verse poems, which is defined as an open form of poetry, which in its modern arose from the French *vers libre* form. It does not use consistent meter patterns, rhyme, or any musical patterns. It tends to follow the rhythm of natural speech.

With that said, please enjoy this new addition called "dance in the rain".

Welcome to Japan !

WELCOME TO JAPAN 1

1

Tokyo Night

In the heart of Tokyo, as the city sleeps
A love story unfolds, delicate and deep
Beneath the neon lights and starlit sky
Two souls entwined, never wanting to say goodbye

In the crowded streets, they find their way
Lost in each other, lost in the fray
Their language echoes through the night
A symphony of joy, a pure delight

Hand in hand, they wander on
Through gardens and shrines, until the dawn
Each moment cherished, each touch divine
In the city of dreams, their love is strong

As the night fades into a new day
Their love story continues, come what may
In Tokyo, where magic and love collide
Their hearts forever intertwined.

2

Sakura

Under the cherry blossom tree, pink petals gently fall like
snowflakes in the springtime sky.
The air is filled with a sweet, fragrant scent that lingers
long after the blooms have faded.
Sakura blossoms, delicate and fleeting, reminding us of
the beauty in impermanence.
They bloom for just a moment, a brief but magical time
before they disappear.
But in that moment, we are captivated by their grace,
their softness, their tranquility.
Sakura blossoms, a reminder of the cycles of life
of growth, of renewal.
And as they fall to the ground, we are reminded that
even in endings, there is beauty.

3

Ode to Thee!

Ode to the man I love,
With eyes that shine like stars above,
His laughter fills my heart with joy,
His touch my soul it does employ.

His kindness like a gentle breeze,
His love a comfort that will ease,
Through trials and triumphs, he stands by me,
A pillar of strength, for all to see.

In his embrace, I will find my peace,
My worries and fears, they all release,
His presence like a warm embrace,
A guiding light, a steady pace.

Ode to the man I love,
Forever grateful to the heavens above,
For sending me this gift so true,
For blessing me with a love so pure.

4

Twilight in Japan

As the sun dips low in a fiery embrace,

Colors dance, painting the sky's face.

A twilight canvas, a celestial art,

In the hush of evening, it steals the heart.

The horizon ignites with a golden fire,

In the tranquil moments, we all admire.

Day bids farewell, and stars take their place,

In the tender arms of the sunset's embrace.

A symphony of hues, a fleeting delight,

In the fading daylight, a magical sight.

Nature's grand finale, a celestial ballet,

In the arms of twilight, we find our way.

5

Love of Tokyo

In a city of neon lights and ancient temples,
I found my heart in the bustling streets of Tokyo.
The frenetic energy, the vibrant colors,
They all captured my soul and made me whole.

From the tranquil gardens of Shinjuku Gyoen,
To the bustling markets of Tsukiji Fish Market,
Every corner of this city holds a piece of my heart,
And I know that Tokyo will always be a part of me.

The cherry blossoms in spring, the snowfall in winter,
Each season brings its own beauty and wonder.
I walk through the crowded streets, lost in thought,
Feeling the pulse of this city, feeling alive.

In Tokyo, I found a love like no other,
A love that transcends time and distance.
And as I leave this place, my heart heavy with longing,
I know that Tokyo will always be my true home.

6

Lady in the White Mask

Behind each face, a story to conceal,
Masks she wears, emotions she conceals.
In the masquerade of life she plays her part,
Yet the truth within, a work of art.

Beneath the laughter and the painted grace,
Lies the complexity of the human race. Each
mask she wears, a different role she casts,
In this intricate drama, life's stage is vast.

We hide our fears and dreams
from sight,
Beneath the layers, in the
day and night.
But in the stillness,
when the masks descend,
Her true self emerges,
with no pretend.

7

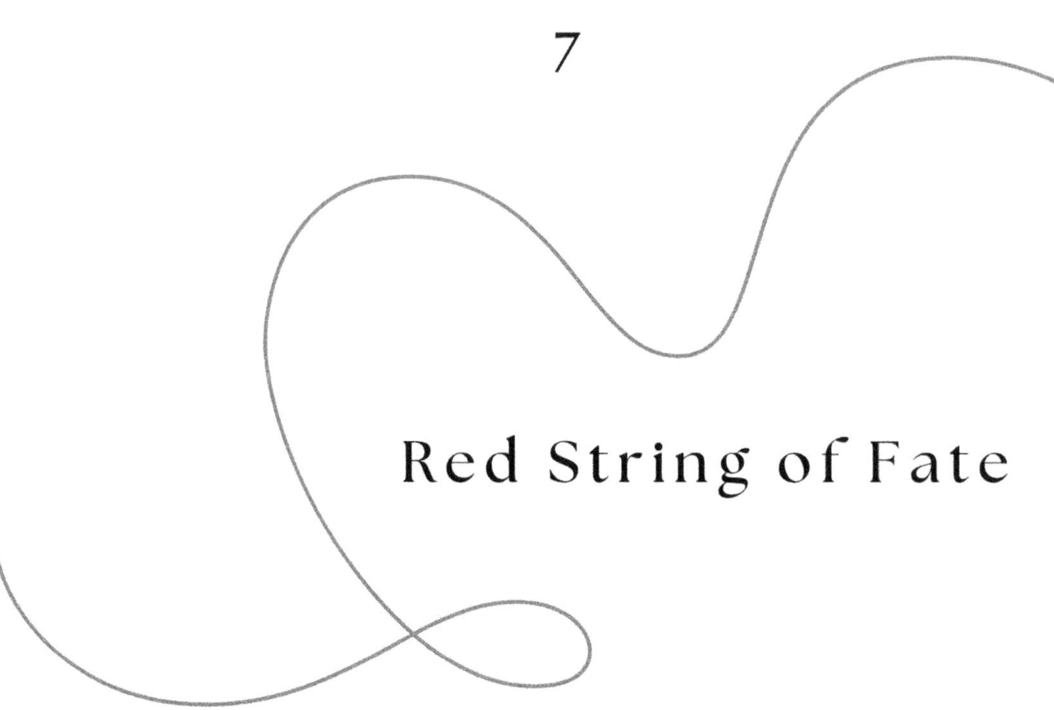

Red String of Fate

In the tapestry of life, a line does weave,
A thread of fate, in what we believe.

It's a line of two lovers, a guide in the dark,
A single thread, where we leave our mark.

To horizons, where dreams take flight,
In the thread of fate, we find our light.

So, in life's journey, remember the line,
The thread of fate, that we all entwine.

It connects our hearts, our spirits in sync,
A symbol of courage, in how we all think.

**Two people connected by the red thread are destined lovers, regardless of place, time or circumstances. **.

8

When We First Met

When we first met, it was as if fate had planned
Our paths to cross, our destinies entwined,
In that fleeting moment, our hearts did expand,
And from that day forth, a journey defined.

Your eyes, a mirror to my soul they seemed,
Reflecting back the love I longed to find,
With every word you spoke, my heart just beamed,
Enraptured by your charm, so sweet and kind.

We walked together, hand in hand, so free,
Exploring love's uncharted territory,
Each step we took, a testament to we,
A partnership bound by sweet harmony.

When we first met, it felt like coming home,
A place of solace, where our love can roam.

9

Dance in the Rain

dance in the rain, feeling free
kiss the one who means the world to me
let the drops fall upon our skin
as we let our inhibitions thin

our hearts beat in the rhythm with the storm
as we dance together, keeping warm
in each other's arms, we find solace
in this moment, nothing else matters

the world fades away as we embrace
each touch, each kiss, each whispered phrase
in this rainfall, we find bliss
dancing in the rain, sharing a kiss

so let the storm rage on outside
for in each other, we'll always find
a love that's true, a love that's real
dancing in the rain, our hearts reveal.

10

Princess of Japan

In the land of cherry blossoms, she reigns

The princess of Japan, noble and serene

Graceful in her kimono, adorned with jewels

Her presence commands respect and admiration

Born into a world of tradition and honor

She upholds her duties with grace and poise

A symbol of purity and beauty, a beacon of light

Guiding her people with wisdom and compassion

Through wars and turmoil, she remains strong

A symbol of resilience and fortitude

Her spirit unyielding, her heart pure

The princess of Japan, a timeless treasure

In her eyes, the history of her ancestors unfolds

Generations of strength and sacrifice

A legacy to uphold, a duty to fulfill

The princess of Japan, a symbol of peace and harmony

May her reign be long and prosperous

May her people find peace and unity

In the presence of their beloved princess

The pride of Japan, for all eternity.

Cherry Blossoms

Pink petals falling

Whispers of spring in the air

Cherry blossoms drift

Strawberry Delight

Juicy red treasure

Sweetness burst with each bite taken

Spring's delight in hand

Bloom in Spring

Blossoms unfurl wide

Colors dancing in the breeze

Spring's warmth brings new life

Tokyo Blossoms

Cherry blossoms bloom

Tokyo's streets are lined with pink

Springtime's beauty shines

Temples

Ancient temples stand

Silent guardians of time

Whispers of the past

Tokyo District

In Tokyo's district

Neon lights illuminate

A city's heartbeat

Tokyo Princess

Elegant Princess

In Tokyo's bustling streets

Graceful as cherry blossoms

Osaka, I Miss You

Gentle Cherry Blossoms

Whispers of Osaka's dream

Longing in my heart

Kyoto Temples

Cherry blossoms bloom

Kyoto memories linger

Peaceful temple grounds

These Haikus are limited not only to Tokyo. But fall into the beauty within the cities.

14

Japanese Love

In the cherry bloom
Japanese lover whispers
Eternal devotion

Devotion

Devotion so pure
A love that knowns no limits
Heart full of flowers

Shinjuku

In Shinjuku's lights
Lost in a sea of people
Urban heartbeat pounds

Serenity

Serenity finds me
In the calm of nature's arms
Peaceful and at rest

Busy Tokyo

In busy Tokyo
Crossing streets full of color
Cherry Blossoms fall

Sakura Kiss

Petals unfurl bright
Sunlight kisses eager buds
Blooming with delight

Taiko

Bating drums in time
Taiko's rhythm fills the air
Heartbeat of Japan

Japan's Countryside

Among rice fields green
Cherry blossoms gently fall
Peaceful countryside

Mt. Fuji

Snow-capped Mt. Fuji
Rising tall into the sky
Sacred beauty shines

17

Miyajima Island

Miyajima Island
Sacred deer roam with grace
Floating torii gate

Senso-ji

Senso-ji temple
Ancient whispers in the wind
Peaceful sanctuary

Hirosaki Castle

Hirosaki Castle
Ancient beauty stands still strong
Cherry blossom blooms

18

Ashikaga Spring Festival

Blooming spring flowers
Ashikaga blossoms fill the air
Spring festival's delight

Kinkaku-ji

Golden temple shrines
Reflecting sunlight's embrace
Kinkaku-ji's grace

Yokote Kamakura

Snow cave in the night
Yokote Kamakura shrines bright
Warmth in winter's bite

Koi Fish

Koi swims gracefully
Through waters cam and serene
Beauty in motion

Hanabi

Colorful bursts high
Light up the dark night sky
Fireworks delight

Forest Spirits

Amidst Japanese trees
Whispers of ancient spirits
Peaceful harmony

Nagano

In Nagano snow
Silent mountains stand proud tall
Nature's quiet call

Yokaichi Old Town

Pristine Yokaichi
Echoes of ancient footsteps
Whispers through the streets

Sawara, Chiba

Soft waves gently crash
Ocean breeze kisses my cheek
Sawara, serene village

MEMORIES OF JAPAN 2

21

I remember...

I remember Japan, so vivid in my mind,
The cherry blossoms blooming, so gentle and one of a kind.
The temples stood tall, with history so rich,
The beauty of the culture, a seamless stitch.

Kyoto's streets, alive with hustle and bustle,
The scent of green tea, a subtle tussle.
Mount Fuji's grandeur, towering above,
A symbol of strength, a beacon of love.

The food, oh the food, a culinary delight,
Sushi and ramen, filling me with pure delight.
The people, so polite, so gracious and kind,
Leaving a lasting impression, in my heart they bind.

I remember Japan, with longing in my heart,
A place of magic and wonder, never to part.
The memories linger, like a sweet lingering song,
Japan, forever in my soul, where I truly belong.

22

Broken Heart

On the day I met Japan, my heart felt whole again,
The beauty of the land, the culture, the zen.
The cherry blossoms blooming, the temples so serene,
Every moment spent there, a memory to be seen.

I wandered through the streets, losing track of time,
The hustle and bustle, a rhythm so sublime.
The kindness of the people, the food, the saké,
I knew in that moment, my heart had found its way.

Japan, oh Japan, you healed my broken soul,
With every step I took, I felt more whole.
The history, the art, the traditions so grand,
Forever in my heart, in my soul, you will stand.

So thank you, Japan, for showing me the light,
For helping me find peace, for making everything right.
I will cherish the memories, hold them close to my chest,
For on the day I met you, my heart was truly blessed.

23
Who am I . . .

In the tranquil pond where lilies bloom,

The beautiful koi glide through the gloom.

Their scales shimmer in the sunlight's glow,

Reflecting colors from the rainbow.

Who am I to witness such grace,

In this serene and sacred place?

A mere observer in the grand design,

Of creatures both tender and divine.

Yet here I stand, in awe and wonder,

At the sight of the koi, who gracefully ponder,

Their purpose in this world so vast,

Their beauty a reminder of the past.

Who am I to question or judge,

These creatures who do not hold a grudge?

I am but a humble soul,

In the presence of something whole.

The beautiful koi, a symbol of peace,

Their movements graceful, never to cease.

Who am I to understand,

The mysteries of this sacred land?

24

Soul Food

In Japan, where seasons bloom and sway with grace,
The soul is fed by food that fills a place
Deep within, beyond the hunger of the belly,
It nourishes the spirit, pure and steady.

From tender slices of sashimi, raw and fresh,
To steaming bowls of miso, warm and meshed,
Each bite is like a tranquil meditation,
A quiet moment of appreciation.

The delicate dance of flavors on the tongue,
A symphony of tastes that leaves me hung
In awe of nature's beauty, artistry,
In every bite, I taste divinity.

So let me dine on sushi, rice, and tea,
And find my soul in Japan's culinary
Delights, where every dish is a work of art,
And every meal feeds both body and heart.

25

Heart of Japan

In the heart of Japan, a land so fair,
Where cherry blossoms bloom in gentle breeze,
Mountains rise and rivers flow with ease,
Peace and harmony fill the air.

The temples stand in silent reverence,
Guardians of a culture rich and old,
Stories of the past forever told,
in whispers of a thousand years existence.

From bustling cities to tranquil shores,
Traditions and modernity collide,
In harmony, a delicate dance dos reside,
A culture preserved, forevermore.

In the heart of Japan, a nation strong,
Where beauty and tradition belong.

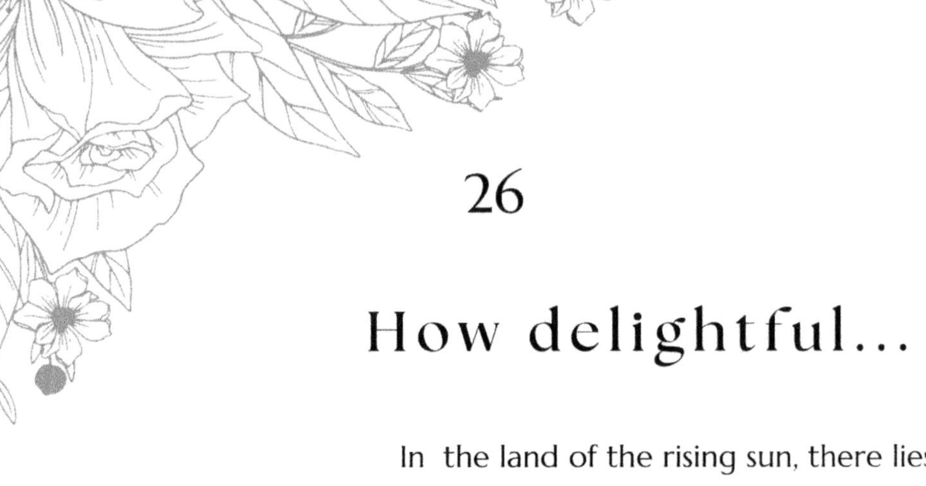

26

How delightful...

In the land of the rising sun, there lies

A cuisine so delicate, so refined.

The food of Japan, a feast for the eyes

And senses, leaving all worries behind.

Sushi and sashimi, fresh from the sea,

Rice and noodles, a staple in every meal

Tempura an teriyaki, oh how heavenly

Each bite, a symphony that makes your heart feel delight.

Matcha and mochi, sweet treats abound,

Green tree and sake, to wash it all down

The flavors of Japan, so pure and profound

In each dish, a story of tradition is found.

From street vendor stalls to Michelin stars,

The food of Japan is a work of art

A celebration of culture, both near and far

A culinary journey that will never depart.

27

Fireworks at Night

In the land of the rising sun, fireworks crackle

An spectacle of light and sound, painting the sky

With vibrant colors, bursting into life

Each explosion a dance, a moment of awe

As they float and fade, drifting back to Earth

The crowd below gasps, in wonder and delight

A tradition passed down through generations

Celebrating the beauty of life, in all its glory

Fireworks in Japan, a symbol of joy

And a reminder of the fleeting nature of existence..

28

Trip of a Lifetime
-2016 from Canada to Japan

In Japan, a land of ancient tradition,

I embarked on a journey of a lifetime.

From bustling Tokyo to serene Kyoto,

Each city held its own unique allure.

The cherry blossoms bloomed in dazzling hues,

As I wandered through historic temples.

The taste of sushi on my lips, divine,

And tea ceremonies steeped in grace and poise.

I gazed in awe at Mount Fuji's grandeur,

And soaked in hot springs beneath starlit skies.

The neon lights of Shibuya dazzled,

While ancient shrines stood silently nearby.

On this trip of a lifetime to Japan,

I found my heart forever changed and full.

The memories I've made will never fade,

A love for this enchanting land, forever entwined.

29

Torii Gates

In Japan, the Torii gates stand tall and proud,
Symbols of the ancient Shinto faith,
Guiding visitors through sacred grounds,
Where prayers are whispered and blessings sought.

Made of wood or stone, they mark the entrance,
To shrines and temples nestled in nature's embrace,
Each gate a portal to a spiritual world,
Where the divine and mortal realms intertwine.

Beneath the crimson arches, time stands still,
A hush descends, a reverence in the air,
As footsteps echo on the winding paths,
Leading to places of peace and contemplation.

The Torii gates, guardians of tradition,
A link to Japan's storied past,
An invitation to all who wander near,
To pause, reflect, and connect with something greater.

30

Ancient Temples

In ancient Japan, temples rise in grace,

Tall towers reaching up to touch the sky.

Their curved roofs sheltered by the heavens' embrace,

A place of peace where troubles seem to fly.

The cherry blossoms bloom in softest hue,

And lanterns cast a warm and gentle light.

Inside, the incense fills the air anew,

As monks in prayer chant softly through the night.

Each wooden beam has stood for centuries,

Whispering stories of a time long past.

The sacred grounds hold ancient memories,

Of samurai and geisha, meant to last.

So wander through these temples, old and wise,

And feel the spirit of Japan arise.

Tokyo is the heart of Japan, as it is the capital city. The poems above
are some food, events and locations in Tokyo, that I love.

WHEN IN KYOTO 3

31

Ebisu-jinja Shrine

In the heart of Tokyo, Ebisu-jinja Shrine stands,

A sanctuary of peace, surrounded by bustling streets.

Devoted to Ebisu, the god of fishermen and fortune,

Its charm and grace attract visitors from far and wide.

Beneath the towering trees, prayers are whispered,

Offerings of coins and sake left at the altar.

A gentle breeze carries the scent of incense,

And the sound of temple bells fills the air.

Ancient rituals are performed with reverence,

Bowing heads and clasped hands in solemn prayer.

The torii gate stands as a symbol of purity,

A gateway to the divine and a line to the past.

In the silence of the shrine, a sense of calm descends,

And for a moment, the world outside fades away.

Ebisu-jinja Shrine, a place of tranquility and grace,

A timeless oasis in the heart of the city.

So wander through these temples, old and wise,

And feel the spirit of Japan arise.

32

Setsubun

In Japan, Setsubun marks the end of winter,
A time to banish evil spirits and welcome spring.
Families come together to throw beans,
Symbolizing the purifying of their homes and hearts.

The sound of laughter fills the air,
As children chase away imaginary demons,
And elders smile at the traditions passed down,
From generation to generation.

With each bean thrown, a wish is made,
For good luck and prosperity in the coming year,
A fresh start as the days grow longer,
And the promise of new beginnings.

And so we celebrate Setsubun,
A time of renewal and hope,
A reminder that darkness fades,
And light will always return.

33

Higashiyama Hanatoro

In the ancient streets of Higashiyama Hanatoro,

lanterns dance with golden glow,

illuminating the path of old,

where stories of the past are told.

Cherry blossoms bloom in soft embrace,

casting shadows on the ancient space,

whispers of a time long gone,

where memories linger on and on.

Each lantern tells a story true,

of love, of loss, of skies so blue,

a tapestry of time unfurled,

in the quiet of this ancient world.

As night falls and stars appear,

Higashiyama Hanatoro draws near,

a reminder of the beauty found,

in the quiet of this hallowed ground.

So walk with me, hand in hand,

through lantern-lit streets we'll stand,

in awe of this timeless art,

in Higashiyama Hanatoro's heart.

34

Kitano Odori Geisha Dance

In the heart of Kyoto's ancient streets

Graceful movements of the Geisha's feet

A dance of beauty and tradition,

Kitano Odori, a captivating rendition

Whispers of silk and delicate fans,

Intricate steps and elegant hands

Each movement tells a story untold,

A spectacle to behold

Under the cherry blossoms' bloom

The Geisha gracefully fills the room

Her presence commands attention,

A symbol of refined perfection

Kitano Odori, a dance of grace

In a world of simple elegance, a sacred place

Where time stands still, and spirits soar,

In the ancient artistry of the Geisha's lore

35

Yabusame Shinji

Upon the field of honor, Yabusame Shinji rides,

A master of the bow, his spirit never hides.

With focus and precision, his arrows take flight,

Guided by ancient tradition, he soars through the night.

The target stands before him, a challenge laid bare,

With grace and determination, he takes careful aim there.

His movements are fluid, like a dancer in the wind,

Each shot a testament to the strength within.

The crowd holds its breath, watching in awe,

As Yabusame Shinji proves his skill once more.

His arrows find their mark, a symphony of sound,

Echoing through the air, a victory profound.

For in this sacred ritual, he is more than a man,

He is a warrior, a hero, a legend in the land.

His name will live on, in stories and in song,

Yabusame Shinji, forever strong.

36

Aoi Matsuri

In the ancient city of Kyoto,

where cherry blossoms bloom

and temples whisper stories of old,

the Aoi Matsuri takes place.

A festival of tradition and beauty,

where dancers in elegant robes

parade through the streets,

offering prayers for a bountiful harvest.

The sound of taiko drums fills the air,

as the procession moves with grace,

a river of green and purple silk

flowing through the ancient capital.

Horses adorned with golden ornaments,

carry the shrine of the Kamo gods,

blessing the city with prosperity

and protection for the year ahead.

Under the shadow of the mountains,

the Aoi Matsuri lives on,

a timeless celebration of Kyoto's rich history,

a reminder of the beauty and grace that endures.

37

Kyoten

In the heart of the forest, hidden away
lies the sacred Kyoten, a place of peace
where cherry blossoms bloom in harmony
and whispers of the past linger in the breeze

Ancient stones tell tales of fallen leaves
while moss-covered pathways lead the way
to a world untouched by time's cruel hand
where nature's beauty holds sway

Here, beneath the canopy of green
the spirit of the land finds its rest
a place of stillness and tranquility
where weary souls can be truly blessed

So let us walk these hallowed grounds
and feel the wisdom of the trees
for in the heart of Kyoten's embrace
we find a sanctuary, a place of ease.

38

Autumn Moon Viewing

In the crisp night air
Beneath the autumn moon's gentle glow
We gather together, a sense of peace
As the leaves whisper their final farewell

The moonlight dancing on the water
Reflecting our hopes and dreams
We speak of love and loss
In the soft embrace of darkness

The beauty of this moment
Fills our hearts with gratitude
For the fleeting nature of life
And the eternal cycle of seasons

Our souls are stirred
By the magic of this night
As we bask in the glow
Of the autumn moon's soft light.

39

Jidai Matsuri

In ancient Kyoto, the streets come alive
With the sound of drums and laughter ringing
Jidai Matsuri, a festival of history

Processions of nobles and warriors clad
In vibrant silks and shining armor
A parade of generations past

A time to honor the traditions of old
To celebrate the beauty of Japan's heritage
In the heart of the city, under autumn skies

The wind whispers secrets of times gone by
As the procession winds its way through the streets
A tapestry of colors, a dance of memories

Jidai Matsuri, a festival of the ages
A celebration of the past, a reminder of the present
In Kyoto, where history lives on.

40

Arashiyama Hanatoro

In Arashiyama's glow,

Hanatoro blossoms bloom,

Guiding souls through the night,

A path of light weaving through the gloom.

Lanterns dance in the breeze,

Casting shadows on the trees,

Whispers of ancient tales,

Echoes of love and bravery.

The river sings a lullaby,

As we walk along the way,

In the gentle embrace of night,

Finding peace in each passing ray.

Arashiyama's beauty unfolds,

In the Hanatoro's light,

A tapestry of dreams and wishes,

A symphony of nature's might.

The poems above are historical places found in Japan.
Great places to visit in Kyoto and names of events that occur in Kyoto.

WHEN IN OSAKA 4

Tako-yaki

Sizzling on the grill
Savory bites of delight
Takoyaki blissful

Okonomiyaki

Flipping on the grill
Okonomiyaki sizzles
Tasty Japanese treat

Ramen

Slurping noodles hot,
Savory broth warms the soul,
Ramen comfort food.

When in Osaka, you must enjoy great street food. These are my favorites..

42

Kushi-katsu

Fried on a stick
Sauce dripping, crunchy delight
Kushi-katsu bliss

TAKOPA (Takoyaki Park)

Takoyaki sizzles
Golden balls of joy beckon
Park of savory delight

Yaekatsu

A gentle breeze blows
Yaekatsu's beauty shines bright
Nature's gift to us

When in Osaka, don't forget to visit historical places.

43

Venture to Osaka

Thanks Osaka, you're quite a sight,

Your beauty shines so bright.

From temples to neon lights,

You fill us with delight.

Thanks for making our stay just right!

Festivity

In Osaka, the festivals are grand

With performances and food so grand

From cherry blossoms blooming

To dancers a-moving

It's a celebration in this vibrant land.

44

Osaka Castle Museum

There once was a castle in Osaka,

Where history was kept for the masa.

With artifacts old,

And stories untold,

The Castle Museum was a true masa.

45

Tomb of Emperor Nintoku (Daisen Kofun)

Upon the lush green land of Japan's isle,

There lies a tomb of grandeur and of grace,

The final resting place of Emperor Nintoku,

A ruler revered by all in his time.

Daisen Kofun, the largest of its kind,

Stands proud and tall, a symbol of his reign,

A testament to his power and his might,

A legacy that echoes through the years.

The earth below holds secrets untold,

Of a leader wise and just, beloved by all,

Whose memory lives on in the hearts of the people,

As they gaze upon his tomb with reverence.

Emperor Nintoku, a man of strength and honor,

His spirit lingers still in the ancient stones,

Guarding his kingdom from beyond the grave,

A silent sentinel of a bygone age.

46

Tsutenkaku Tower

In Osaka stands the Tsutenkaku Tower tall,
A beacon of history and beauty in the bustling city.
Its steel frame reaching for the skies,
A symbol of resilience and strength.

Built in the early 20th century,
A monument to progress and innovation.
Visitors from far and wide come to see,
The breathtaking views from the top.

From its observation deck,
One can see the city stretch out below.
The bustling streets and neon lights,
A vibrant tapestry of modern life.

But amidst the hustle and bustle,
The Tsutenkaku Tower stands serene.
A reminder of the past and the present,
A testament to the enduring spirit of Osaka.

47

Ganko Hiranogo Yashiki

In the shadows of Ganko Hiranogo Yashiki,
Where stories of the past still linger in the air,
Whispers of ghosts haunt the grand old estate,
Echoes of samurais and geishas from days gone by.

The walls hold secrets, the floors bear witness,
To the love and loss, the joy and sorrow,
Of those who once called this place their home,
Their presence still felt in every room.

Silent gardens filled with cherry blossoms,
Tell tales of romance and betrayal,
The beauty of the flowers a stark contrast,
To the darkness that lurks within the walls.

As night falls, the spirits come alive,
Dancing in the moonlight, weaving their tales,
A tapestry of memories and regrets,
That will never be forgotten in Ganko Hiranogo Yashiki.

48

Life in Osaka

In Osaka, where the city never sleeps,

The neon lights flicker and dance in the streets.

A bustling hub of culture and life,

Where traditions blend with modern strife.

The cherry blossoms bloom in the spring,

As the people gather and laugh and sing.

From historic castles to high-tech thrills,

Osaka's energy never stands still.

The food is rich, the flavors bold,

From takoyaki to ramen, a feast for the soul.

The markets hum with vendors' calls,

As tourists wander through ancient walls.

In Osaka, where the river flows,

There's a rhythm to life that everyone knows.

The pace is fast, the hearts are warm,

In this vibrant city, where dreams are born.

49

To live in Osaka. . .

In the heart of Japan lies Osaka, bustling city

Where cherry blossoms bloom and temples stand tall

The neon lights shine bright in the night

And the streets are alive with the hustle and bustle

To live in Osaka is to taste the flavors of the world

From takoyaki to ramen, sushi to okonomiyaki

The food scene is vibrant and diverse

A culinary adventure for the taste buds

In Osaka, tradition meets modernity

Ancient shrines next to skyscrapers

Geishas walking alongside salarymen

A juxtaposition of old and new

To live in Osaka is to embrace the culture

To learn the language, the customs, the way of life

To be a part of a city that never sleeps

Where every corner holds a new discovery

So if you find yourself in Osaka one day

Embrace the chaos, the beauty, the energy

For to live in Osaka is to live fully

In a city that never fails to amaze.

50

Osaka Traditions

In Osaka, ancient traditions still thrive,
Passed down through generations with great pride.
The tea ceremony, elegant and refined,
Held in tranquil gardens, a serene find.

The temples stand tall, with their pagoda roofs,
Echoing chants of priests, a timeless truth.
The festivals, with their vibrant displays,
Celebrating culture in colorful ways.

Sumo wrestlers grapple in the sacred ring,
Honoring ancestors in this ancient thing.
From kabuki theater to the art of bonsai,
Osaka's traditions never fade or die.

So let us cherish and protect these ways,
For they are what make Osaka truly praise.
May our heritage shine for all to see,
In the heart of this city, proud and free.

51

The Art of Japanese Cuisine

In the land of the rising sun, where cherry blossoms bloom,
Lies a treasure trove of flavors, beyond the kitchen room.
The art of Japanese cuisine, a feast for both the eyes and soul,
Where every dish is a masterpiece, carefully crafted and whole.

Sushi, sashimi, tempura, and ramen galore,
Each bite a symphony of taste, leaving you wanting more.
The delicate balance of flavors, the precision in each cut,
Shows the dedication and love, behind each Japanese chef.

From miso soup to matcha tea, each ingredient sings,
Of the centuries-old tradition, that Japan proudly brings.
The beauty of Japanese cuisine, lies not just in the taste,
But in the artistry and honor, with which it is embraced.

So let us raise our chopsticks, and toast to this cuisine,
For the beauty of Japanese food, is like nothing we've seen.
A culinary journey, a feast for both the heart and mind,
Japanese cuisine will forever captivate, for it is truly one of a kind.

52

Miso soup

Miso soup, a bowl of comfort and warmth,
A savory broth with seaweed and tofu,
Each spoonful a taste of umami delight.
Simple yet complex, a depth of flavor,
A nourishing meal for body and soul.

The miso paste dissolves into the hot water,
Releasing its rich and complex essence,
A blend of soybeans, rice, and salt,
Fermented to perfection, a work of art.
The floating tofu, firm and silky,
Absorbing the flavors of the broth,
A delicate balance of textures and tastes.

Seaweed dances in the bowl, crisp and green,
Adding a touch of the ocean's essence,
A hint of brine to complement the richness.
Each sip brings comfort and satisfaction,
A moment of peace in a busy world,
Miso soup, a simple pleasure to savor.

53

Udon Soup

In a bowl of Udon soup, noodles stretch long and thin
Slurped up with satisfaction, warmth seeping into skin
Broth rich with flavor, comforting and bold
Topped with scallions, a sight to behold

A taste of Japan in every spoonful taken
Umami essence, leaving taste buds awaken
Vegetables floating, adding color and crunch
A symphony of ingredients, in perfect lunch

Udon soup, a simple yet complex delight
Each ingredient dancing, creating a harmonious sight
Savoring each bite, in a quiet moment of peace
Finding solace in the warmth, as worries cease.

54

Yakitori

In the heart of Japan, under the glowing lights
Of paper lanterns and lively chatter,
Yakitori sizzles on the grill,
Skewered pieces of succulent chicken,
Marinated in sweet soy and fragrant spices.
The aroma fills the bustling street,
Drawing in passersby with its enticing scent.
Each bite is a burst of flavor,
Juicy and tender, perfectly charred.
A culinary delight that brings joy to all who taste it.
Yakitori, a culinary masterpiece,
Simple yet exquisite in its execution.
An art form in itself,
A celebration of the humble chicken,
Transformed into a dish fit for a king.
So next time you find yourself in Japan,
Seek out a quaint yakitori stall,
And immerse yourself in the magic
Of this delicious and unforgettable treat.

55

Donburi

Upon a bed of rice, a meal is made,

Donburi, a dish of simplicity,

Yet bursting with flavors in every bite.

A bowl filled with ingredients so diverse,

From tender meat to vegetables so fresh,

Topped with an egg, with yolk so rich and warm,

Each spoonful brings a taste that warms the soul.

Soy sauce and mirin blend in perfect harmony,

Creating a sauce that coats each grain of rice.

Oh, Donburi, you are a culinary delight,

A humble bowl that brings such pure delight.

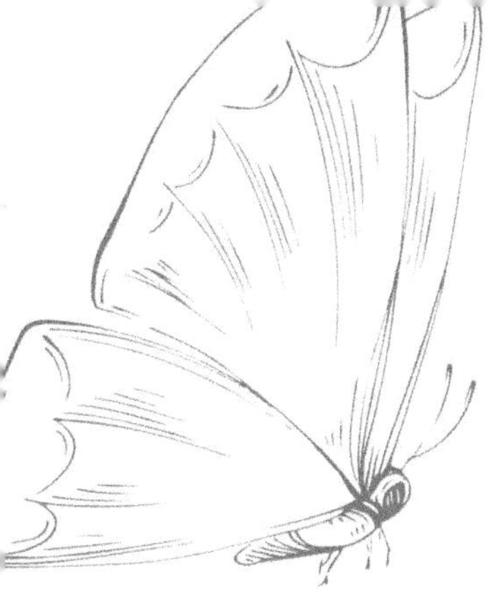

56

Tonkatsu

In a flurry of golden breadcrumbs,
Plump pork cutlets sizzle in hot oil,
Aromas of umami and tangy sauce
Filling the air with promises of comfort.

Crisp and tender, each bite is a symphony
Of flavors and textures, a harmonious dance
Of savory meat and crunchy coating,
A gastronomic delight on a plate.

Tonkatsu, beloved Japanese dish,
Bringing joy and satisfaction to all
Who indulge in its simple yet decadent
Pleasures, a culinary treasure to behold.

57

Tamagoyaki

I stand at the kitchen counter, whisk in hand
Ready to create the perfect Tamagoyaki
Eggs beaten with a gentle touch
A dash of soy sauce for flavor
I pour the mixture into the rectangular pan
Watching as it begins to cook
Slowly roll the edges in towards the center
Layer by layer, building the perfect roll
The sweet and savory scent fills the air
As I carefully slice into the golden roll
Each bite melts in my mouth
A taste of tradition and comfort
Tamagoyaki, a simple dish with a complex history
A symbol of patience and precision
Each layer a testament to the care
Put into creating something beautiful
I savor each bite, grateful for this moment
Lost in the art of cooking
Tamagoyaki, a simple pleasure
That brings warmth to the soul.

58

Kushi-Katsu

In the heart of Osaka's streets, a savory delight,

Kushikatsu sizzles on the grill, a tempting sight.

Skewers of meats and veggies, dipped in batter light,

Deep-fried to perfection, a flavor dynamite.

Dipped in tangy sauce, a symphony of taste,

Crunchy on the outside, tender on the inside, no waste.

Each bite a revelation, a culinary grace,

Kushikatsu is a dish that never goes to waste.

From hole-in-the-wall joints to fancy restaurants dressed in light,

Kushikatsu brings people together, a culinary delight.

So next time you're in Osaka, don't hesitate, take a bite,

Of this fried perfection, a true culinary sight.

59

Dotonbori in Osaka

In the heart of Osaka lies Dotonbori,
Where neon lights illuminate the night.
A bustling street of shops and restaurants,
Where tourists and locals alike unite.

The Glico Running Man, an iconic sight,
Bridges span across the Dotonbori Canal.
Crowds gather around to take in the view,
As lively sounds of laughter fill the air.

Food stalls line the streets, offering delights,
Takoyaki, okonomiyaki, and more.
The aroma of delicious dishes wafts,
Drawing hungry patrons to explore.

The energy of Dotonbori never fades,
A vibrant hub of culture, fun, and flair.
An unforgettable experience awaits,
In Osaka's lively and bustling square.

These poems feature some of my favorite food, locations and attractions in Osaka. Things I recommend everyone to check out.

WHEN IN TOKYO 5

60

When in Tokyo...

In Tokyo, the city of bright lights and bustling streets,

Where ancient tradition meets modern feats,

A whirlwind of culture and vibrant energy,

A land of sushi, temples, and cherry blossoms aplenty.

The neon signs that light up the night,

Guide us through this concrete jungle with delight,

Skyscrapers towering high above,

Reflecting the dreams of those who dare to love.

Streets filled with a mix of old and new,

Where each corner holds a fresh view,

From tranquil gardens to crowded crosswalks,

Every experience leaves us in awe.

In Tokyo, the rhythm of the city beats strong,

A harmony of chaos that pulls us along,

We lose ourselves in its vibrant embrace,

And leave with memories we can never replace.

Nigiri-zushi

Fresh fish on rice bed
Wasabi, soy sauce enhance
Nigiri-zushi joy

Chankonabe

Steam rising above
Chankonabe fills the air
Sumo warriors feast

Monjayaki

Sizzling on the grill
Monjayaki delights all
Tokyo street food

When in Tokyo, you must enjoy great street food. These are my favorites..

62

Kagurazaka - France Town

In Kagurazaka, a slice of France in Japan,

The cobblestone streets whisper tales of old,

Where traditional meets modern in a seamless blend,

Bistros and boutiques lining the narrow roads.

A quaint town full of charm and grace,

Where cherry blossoms bloom in the spring,

And lanterns light up the night sky,

Creating a magical, romantic scene.

Patisseries with decadent pastries tempt the senses,

And cafes with delicate desserts welcome all,

As the scent of fresh baguettes fills the air,

Inviting you to sit and linger for a while.

In Kagurazaka, time seems to slow down,

As you wander through its picturesque lanes,

A fusion of cultures harmoniously coexisting,

In this haven of beauty and tranquility.

63

Shin Okubo - Koreatown

In Shin Okubo, Koreatown comes alive,

A fusion of tradition and modern flair,

Neon lights illuminate the bustling streets,

Where kimchi and ramen scent the air.

K-pop beats pulse through the crowded lanes,

Fashionistas in trendy threads roam free,

From BBQ joints to karaoke bars,

A vibrant culture for all to see.

The Hanbok meets Harajuku in this place,

Where East meets West in harmonious delight,

A melting pot of flavors, sights, and sounds,

In Shin Okubo, where day turns into night.

So take a stroll down these colorful streets,

Experience a taste of Korea here,

In Shin Okubo, Koreatown's heartbeat,

A vibrant world that always brings us near.

64

Ikebukuro - Chinatown

In Ikebukuro's bustling Chinatown,
Sights and smells come alive on every street,
A tapestry of culture, vibrant and sweet,
Where traditions blend in a harmonious town.

The lanterns hang with a mystical glow,
Guiding visitors through the narrow alleys,
A symphony of flavors, enticing, rousing,
In every bite, an ancient story to know.

From steaming dumplings to crispy bao,
The taste of China fills the busy air,
And as the day fades into the night's care,
The pulse of Ikebukuro begins to slow.

Yet beneath the calm, a heartbeat thrums,
A city alive with tales yet to come,
In Ikebukuro's Chinatown, the past and present become one.

65

Shinjuku Station

Amidst city lights,
Shinjuku Station buzzes,
Trains come and go fast.

Yurakucho Station

Neon lights glowing
In Yurakucho Station
A bustling hub sought

Sensoji Temple in Asakusa

Ancient temple stands
In Asakusa's heart, a shrine
Whispers of the past

66

Marunouchi

In Marunouchi's heart, where bustling crowds flow,
Skyscrapers tower high with grandeur bold,
A fusion of tradition and modern glow,
Lined streets with shops and offices untold.

The pulse of Tokyo beats strong and true,
In Marunouchi's veins, a city's life,
Where past and present seamlessly accrue,
A hub of energy and urban strife.

Amidst the chaos, a calmness can be found,
In quiet corners, history whispers low,
A timeless beauty on familiar ground,
Where dreams and ambitions ebb and flow.

In Marunouchi's embrace, one can feel,
The heartbeat of a city, a vibrant reel.

When in Tokyo, these locations are great outdoor and international food spots.

67

Tokyo is just a dream..

Tokyo is just a dream, a distant place

Where neon lights illuminate the night

And cherry blossoms bloom in springtime grace

A city where tradition meets the modern sight

The bustling streets, the bustling crowds, the noise

Of laughter, conversation, and delight

A place where dreams can be realized, voiced

In the land of the rising sun, so bright

But Tokyo is just a dream, a place

That exists far beyond our reach, our sight

A world of wonder, beauty, and embrace

A place we long to visit, day and night

Yet in our hearts, Tokyo will always gleam

A dream that keeps us hopeful, alive, and unseen.

68

Tsukiji Fish Market

In Tokyo's bustling streets of neon glow,
A city where the ancient merges with the new,
Where cherry blossoms bloom in soft pink hue,
And skyscrapers pierce the sky in perfect row.

The Tsukiji fish market with its lively flow,
A culinary haven for the seafood-loving few,
While Meiji Shrine stands majestic and true,
A place for peaceful retreat from the urban show.

Lost in translation in this concrete maze,
Yet finding beauty in the chaos all around,
Here in Tokyo, where ancient meets modern days,
A city of contrasts, where silence can be found.

Ode to Tokyo, with its unique charm,
A vibrant city that will forever disarm.

69

Meiji Shrine

In the heart of Tokyo stands Meiji Shrine,
A sanctuary of peace and serenity.
The towering torii gates welcome all,
As we leave the city's chaos behind.
The ancient cedar trees guard the path,
Their branches reaching towards the sky above.
A sense of reverence fills the air,
As visitors pay homage to the past.
Emperor Meiji, revered and respected,
A symbol of Japan's modernity and strength.
His legacy lives on in this sacred place,
Where we offer prayers for peace and harmony.
Silent prayers whispered in the breeze,
A connection to something greater than ourselves.
In the quiet stillness of the shrine,
We find solace in the midst of chaos.
Meiji Shrine, a beacon of hope,
Guiding us towards a brighter tomorrow.
In this sacred place, we find refuge,
And a reminder of our shared humanity.

70

Water Lilies

Amidst the tranquil waters they bloom,

Water lilies in ethereal grace,

Their petals delicate, pure as moonlight,

Floating serenely, a vision of calm.

Roots anchored deep in the murky depths,

Yet reaching towards the shimmering light,

Symbols of beauty, resilience, and peace,

A testament to nature's flawless design.

Their leaves unfurl like emerald jewels,

Glistening with dew in the early morn,

A haven for frogs and dragonflies,

A tapestry of life in peaceful repose.

Oh, water lilies, how you enchant,

With your subtle elegance and subtle charm,

A gift from the heavens, a sight to behold,

Forever immortalized in song and art.

71

Dream of Tokyo...

In dreams I wander through Tokyo's streets so bright,

Lost in a world of neon lights that never fade.

I see the cherry blossoms blooming in the park,

And hear the gentle sound of laughter in the air.

The bustling crowds, the trains that never sleep,

The ancient temples hidden in the modern sprawl.

I feel the pulse of this metropolis so alive,

A city where the past and present intertwine.

I climb the towering buildings, reach for the sky,

And watch the sun set over Tokyo Bay.

I close my eyes and breathe in the city's essence,

Knowing that in my dreams, Tokyo will always stay.

72

Secrets

In Tokyo, lights flicker through the night,
A city veiled in secrets hidden deep.
Beneath the bustling streets, a web of lies
And whispers fill the air, a silent keep.
Behind the temples and neon-lit signs,
Unseen by many, tales unfold untold.
The mysteries of ancient times still dwell
Within the city's heart, a story old.
From Geisha dances to samurai dreams,
To whispered promises in alleyways,
The secrets of Tokyo, like cherry blossoms,
Unfold their petals in the gentle haze.
In every corner, whispers softly drift,
Revealing truths that few may ever know.
In Tokyo's heart, the secrets softly shift,
A tapestry of mystery, to show.
So listen closely to the city's call,
For Tokyo holds secrets, one and all.

73

We Will Meet Again

Goodbye Tokyo, we will meet again,

In the land of cherry blossoms so fair.

The memories we made will remain,

In my heart, like a silent prayer.

The bustling streets and neon lights,

The peaceful temples, a sacred sight.

The sushi bars and ramen shops,

The beauty of Mount Fuji, reaching great heights.

So many sights to see, so much to do,

But now it's time to bid adieu.

I'll cherish the moments we shared,

And look forward to the day we'll be there.

Goodbye Tokyo, with your vibrant charm,

I'll hold you close and keep you warm.

Until we meet again, my friend,

Our journey together will never end.

When in Tokyo: these are some of my favorite foods, locations and
attractions in Tokyo. Please visit them.

WHEN IN HOKKAIDO 6

74

When in Hokkaido

When in Hokkaido, the land of snow and sea,

Where mountains rise and forests stretch for miles,

The air is crisp, the scenery breathtaking,

A paradise of beauty, nature's own design.

The cherry blossoms bloom in springtime's hue,

Turning mountainsides into a painted scene,

And in the fall, the leaves ablaze with fire,

A tapestry of color, a sight to admire.

In winter, snows blanket the land in white,

Creating a wonderland, a snowy delight,

The hot springs beckon, a welcome respite,

From the cold winds that blow with all their might.

In Hokkaido, where nature reigns supreme,

Where mountains meet the sea in perfect harmony,

A place of peace, of beauty and of grace,

A land of wonder, a truly special place.

75

Ika-Odori

Ika-Odori dance,
Elegant squid in the sea,
Graceful movement shines.

Hokkai Soran Festival

Hokkai Soran dance
Graceful movements enchant all
Festival delight

Hokkaido Jingu Shrine Festival

Winter festival
Hokkaido Jingu Shrine
Peaceful snow falling

Maruyama Zoo

Maruyama Zoo calls,

Lions roar in the distance,

Nature's harmony.

Shikotsu Lake

Shikotsu Lake gleams bright

Festival lights dance in night

Joyful hearts take flight

77

Sapporo Snow Festival

In Sapporo's city streets, the snow falls softly,

Blanketing the town in a pristine white.

But soon, artists and dreamers unite eagerly,

To carve out sculptures with skill and delight.

Majestic ice castles rise tall and grand,

As visitors marvel at the intricate detail.

Each creation crafted by a talented hand,

Bringing joy to all who brave the winter chill.

The Snow Festival brings laughter and cheer,

As families gather to admire the art.

Children play in the icy wonderland, without fear,

Their joy warming the coldest heart.

And as the sun sets on this magical display,

We bid farewell to another winter's day.

But the memories of this festival will forever stay,

In our hearts, where they will never fade away.

78

Asahikawa Winter Festival

In Asahikawa, where snow falls softly,

The Winter Festival comes to life,

Blankets of white covering the town,

Ice sculptures glisten in the sunlight.

Children's laughter fills the frosty air,

As they slide down icy slopes with glee,

Hot cocoa warms their cold, rosy cheeks,

While fireworks light up the night sky.

Visitors from near and far flock here,

To marvel at the beauty of the season,

Music and dance echo through the streets,

A celebration of winter's magic.

Asahikawa Winter Festival shines bright,

A time of joy, of wonder, of delight.

79

Sapporo Lilac Festival

In Sapporo's vibrant cityscape, blooms the Lilac Festival,
Where delicate petals sway in the gentle spring breeze.
A sea of purple hues, stretching as far as the eye can see,
Creating a scenic wonderland, a feast for the senses.

The air is filled with a sweet, intoxicating fragrance,
Drawing in visitors from far and wide to behold the spectacle.
Families stroll hand in hand, basking in nature's beauty,
Children giggle and play amidst the blossoms, carefree.

As the sun sets, the lilacs glow with a soft, ethereal light,
Casting shadows that dance and play across the ground.
The festival is a celebration of life, of renewal and growth,
A reminder of the beauty that lies all around us.

So let us linger here awhile, in this enchanted garden,
Immersed in the peaceful serenity of the Lilac Festival.
For in these moments, we are reminded of the inherent magic
That lies within nature's embrace, forever and always.

80

Hokkaido Crab

In Hokkaido's icy waters, the crab does dwell,
With claws of strength, they navigate the swell.
Their shells adorned in shades of red and white,
A sight to behold, a majestic sight.

With legs so agile, they scuttle across the sand,
Hunting for food, their mission clear and grand.
Their meat so sweet, a delicacy divine,
Savored by many, a taste so fine.

From the ocean depths, they emerge with grace,
A symbol of Hokkaido, a treasured embrace.
The Hokkaido crab, revered by all,
In every bite, a story to recall.

So let us honor this creature of the sea,
A true masterpiece of nature's decree.
The Hokkaido crab, a wonder to behold,
In every taste, a tale untold.

81

Jingisukan

In Hokkaido where winter winds blow cold,
A dish of lamb grilled on iron plates,
Jingisukan, a feast for young and old,
Sizzling and savory, a meal that satiates.

Thin slices of meat, cooked to perfection,
Marinated in soy and garlic delight,
Tender and juicy, a culinary reflection,
Of Mongolian origins, a taste that ignites.

Gather 'round the table, friends and family near,
Sharing stories and laughter, in warmth and cheer,
Jingisukan brings us together, a meal so dear,
A tradition upheld, year after year.

So raise your chopsticks, toast to this fare,
A blend of cultures, a flavor rare,
Jingisukan, a dish beyond compare,
In the heart of Hokkaido, always there.

82

Amezaiku

Amezaiku, a craft of centuries past,
Where sugar and artistry combine at last,
The skilled hands of the artist deftly mold,
Creating creatures, flowers, stories told.

Soft colors blend, delicate forms take shape,
Amezaiku masterpieces, no one can escape,
From simple animal shapes to complex designs,
Each creation holds magic that forever shines.

Children's eyes widen in wonder and awe,
As they watch the sugar come to life and draw,
The sweetness of the treat matched by the joy,
Of witnessing artistry without alloy.

Amezaiku, a tradition cherished and rare,
A reminder of beauty in a world so spare,
A fleeting moment of sweetness and grace,
Captured in sugar, in this delicate place.

83

Agemono

Agemono, sizzling and tempting, their aroma fills the air,
Golden and crispy, a delight for the senses to bear.
Tempura shrimp, fried to perfection,
A savory treat, a culinary affection.

Eggplant katsu, crunchy and savory,
Each bite a symphony, a taste so savory.
The art of deep frying, a craft refined,
Bringing joy to taste buds, a feast for the mind.

From tonkatsu to karaage, a variety abound,
Each dish unique, a flavor expound.
Agemono, a treasure of Japanese cuisine,
A culinary journey, a delightful scene.

84

Ikayaki

Ikayaki, a Japanese delight, grilled squid

Succulent tentacles, charred to perfection

Served on a stick, with a savory glaze

A street food favorite, enjoyed by many

The aroma wafts through the bustling market

Drawing in crowds with its tempting scent

Each bite a burst of umami goodness

A culinary experience not to be missed

Ikayaki, a simple yet exquisite dish

Bringing joy to all who taste its flavors

A treat to savor, a taste of Japan

Forever etched in memory, forever loved.

85

Taiyaki

In Japan, a sweet treat shaped like a fish,
A taiyaki filled with red bean paste warm,
Its crispy exterior a golden dish,
A comfort food that brings joy and calm.

The scent of baking batter in the air,
Brings memories of festivals and fun,
A simple pleasure beyond compare,
A taste of childhood for everyone.

With each bite, a burst of sweet delight,
Warm and filling, a perfect snack,
Taiyaki, a delicious sight,
A culinary joy we never lack.

So let us savor this tasty dish,
And cherish moments of pure bliss.

86

Karaage

Golden nuggets of crispy perfection,

Karaage, oh how you captivate my taste buds.

Marinated in a sauce of savory soy,

Fried to a perfect crunch that delights.

Each bite, a symphony of flavors,

Juicy chicken encased in a fragrant shell.

Served hot and fresh, a culinary treasure,

A Japanese delight that never fails to satisfy.

Simple yet so satisfying,

Karaage, you are a true comfort food.

With each morsel, I am transported,

To a place of pure gastronomic bliss.

The above poems are all locations, events and great food of Hokkaido.
When in Hokkaido check out these amazing places and food.

87

Beauty of Hokkaido

In Hokkaido's gentle hills and snowy peaks,
The beauty of nature whispers sweetly,
A symphony of colors, a serene retreat,
Where mountains meet the sea in harmony.

The lavender fields stretch out to the horizon,
Their fragrance dancing on the cool, crisp air,
While snow-capped mountains stand tall and proud,
Reflecting the sun's golden morning stare.

In every season, Hokkaido's beauty shines,
From cherry blossoms in the springtime bloom,
To autumn leaves ablaze in fiery hues,
The island's charm will never meet its doom.

Oh Hokkaido, your beauty knows no end,
A paradise of peace and calm transcend.

88

We will meet again...

Goodbye Hokkaido we will meet again,

Your snow-capped peaks and forests lush and green.

The memories we made will forever remain,

In our hearts, a love that's pure and clean.

The gentle lapping of the waves on shore,

The call of birds in skies so blue and bright.

We'll miss the beauty we were blessed to explore,

But know in our hearts, we'll reunite.

The peaceful silence of a winter's morn,

The magic of the cherry blossoms in the spring.

We leave behind, but we're not forlorn,

For Hokkaido, to you, our hearts will always cling.

Goodbye for now, but not forever,

We'll cherish the moments we shared together.

In our minds, you'll always linger,

Goodbye Hokkaido, until we meet again, whenever.

LOVE POEMS 7

89

Love's Embrace

In love's gentle embrace, we find our peace,
A bond so strong, it will never cease.
Through trials and triumphs, we stand as one,
Our hearts entwined until the day is done.

In each other's eyes, we see our truth,
A love so pure, it transcends our youth.
With every touch, our souls ignite,
A flame burning bright in the darkest night.

Through laughter and tears, we weather the storm,
Our love a beacon, keeping us warm.
With whispered words and tender caress,
We find solace in each other's sweet embrace.

So let us cherish this love we've found,
For in each other's arms, we are truly bound.
Forever entwined, hearts beating as one,
In this love we've found, our journey begun.

90

Just a memory...

Our love is a memory,

A delicate whisper in the wind,

Fleeting like a summer breeze,

Gone before we could truly begin.

We danced in the moonlight,

Lost in each other's gaze,

But now all that's left

Are echoes of our days.

I remember your laughter,

Like music to my ears,

But now it's just a ghost,

A fading memory through the years.

Our love was a beautiful flame,

But now it's just a spark,

A bittersweet reminder

Of the passion in our hearts.

Though our love may be a memory,

I'll always hold it dear,

For in those fleeting moments,

Our love was truly sincere.

91

Moonlight Dance

Dance in the moonlight, under the rain,
Each drop a rhythm, a melody to sustain.
The silver glow, a gentle embrace,
As we move together, in this tranquil space.

The world around us fades away,
Leaving only us, in our own ballet.
The pitter-patter of rain, a soothing sound,
Our feet gliding on the wet ground.

Arms outstretched, reaching for the sky,
Our hearts beating in time, as we fly.
In this moment, nothing else exists,
Just you and me, in this midnight mist.

So let us dance, in the moonlight glow,
Under the rain, our spirits aglow.
For in this simple, magical romance,
We find our peace, our blissful trance.

92

Melody of a Lover's Heart

A melody to love, soft and sweet

Floating through the air, gentle and discreet

It whispers of affection, of joy and grace

A harmonious tune that fills the space

Like a lullaby to my weary soul

It wraps me in warmth, makes me whole

Each note a kiss, each chord a hug

Overflowing with tenderness like a gentle tug

It dances in my heart, it sings in my mind

A melody to love, so pure and kind

It brightens my days, it eases my pain

A soothing balm in a world of disdain

So I'll cherish this melody, hold it dear

For in its embrace, I have nothing to fear

A melody to love, a gift from above

Forever in my heart, forever in my love.

Embrace

Embrace of love sweet

Hearts beating as one in peace

Together, we thrive

Beating Hearts

Hearts beating in time

Pulsing with love's rhythm sweet

Two souls intertwined

Souls Intertwined

Two souls intertwined

Bound by love and unity

Eternal connection.

Forever

Eternal embrace

Japanese lover's sweet touch

Forever with you

Eternity

Eternal lover,

Timeless bond unbreakable,

Forever in love.

Serenity of Love

Love's serenity

Calms the storms within my soul

Peace in your embrace

95

My personal love story...

In a world of chaos, we found our own peace,

Two souls entwined, a love that will not cease.

Through trials and tribulations, we held strong,

Our bond grew deeper, our connection long.

From the first glance, I knew you were the one,

My heart beating faster, my mind undone.

Every moment with you feels like a dream,

A love story written in the stars it seems.

Through laughter and tears, we weathered the storm,

Our love shining brightly, forever warm.

Together we face the world, hand in hand,

Our personal love story, oh, so grand.

96

when I was your queen...

When you called me your queen, my heart did swell

With pride and joy, like nothing I had felt

Before, your words so sweet and tender, tell

Me how you cherish me, how I've been dealt

A grander hand than I had ever dreamed

Could be mine, with you, my love, by my side

I stand tall, confident, or so it seemed

When you declare me your queen, full of pride

And honor, I'll wear this title with grace

For you, my king, have crowned me as your own

You make me feel like I'm in the right place

With you, my love, my heart has fully grown

So thank you, my dear, for all that you do

For making me your queen, forever true.

97

Secret Relationship...

Let's have a secret relationship, just between us,

A special bond that only we can share,

Until the day comes when we can be free,

And openly declare our love without a care.

For now, let's steal moments in the shadows,

Whispering sweet nothings in the dark,

Glimpses of our future in our eyes,

A connection that ignites a spark.

I long for the day when we can be together,

No more hiding, no more pretending,

Just two hearts beating as one,

A love story that knows no ending.

Until then, let's cherish this secret bond,

Building a foundation strong and true,

For when the time finally comes,

Our love will shine bright, unbreakable and new.

98

Two Hearts Intertwined

Two hearts intertwined regardless of distance,
Connected by a love that knows no bounds.
Across the miles, their love still persists,
A bond so strong, it echoes sweet sounds.

Though miles may separate them physically,
Their hearts remain joined in unity.
Each beat of one is felt by the other,
Their love enduring, like no other.

Through valleys deep and mountains high,
Their love will carry them through any trial.
No distance can tear them apart,
For their love is a force, a work of art.

So let the miles stretch far and wide,
For their love will always be by their side.
Two hearts intertwined, a love so true,
No distance can break the bond between the two.

99

Japan's Love Story

In ancient Japan, a love story unfolds,

A tale of passion, tradition, and honor,

Two hearts entwined in the cherry blossom groves,

Bound by the ancient rites of courtly love.

She, a gentle maiden of grace and poise,

He, a noble warrior of strength and might,

Their love forbidden by the rigid laws,

Yet burns with the intensity of a thousand suns.

Through hardships and trials, they persevere,

Defying the odds and societal norms,

Their love a beacon in a world of darkness,

A flame that lights the way to a brighter dawn.

Their story whispered in the winds of time,

A testament to the power of true love,

Eternal and unyielding like the rising sun,

Their hearts forever bound in Japan's love story.

100

Do you want to visit Japan?

In the land of rising sun, my heart finds peace,

Amongst cherry blossoms and ancient shrines,

I roam the streets of Tokyo with ease,

In awe of temples and serene inclines.

The love of travel to Japan runs deep,

In every bow, in every cup of tea,

I lose myself in beauty, wide and steep,

In gardens filled with tranquility.

From Mount Fuji to Kyoto's ancient streets,

I wander on in wonder, never bored,

The culture and the history that greets,

Enchants me like a novel yet untold.

Oh Japan, my heart belongs to thee,

In your embrace, I find my soul set free.

101

Land of Peace and Tranquility

In the land of rising sun, serenity reigns,
A peaceful haven amidst chaos and strains.
Cherry blossoms bloom with grace and charm,
Whispers of tranquility, a soothing balm.

Mountains stand tall, in silent majesty,
Cascading waterfalls, a symphony.
Ancient temples dot the verdant landscape,
Silent prayers, a tranquil escape.

The gentle rustle of bamboo leaves,
A sense of calm that never leaves.
Tea ceremonies, a ritual divine,
In every sip, a moment to unwind.

In the beauty of simplicity, Japan excels,
A land of peace, where harmony dwells.
In every corner, a sense of calm,
A gentle refuge, a soothing balm.

102

Do you love Japan?

Do you love Japan? The land of cherry blossoms,
Where ancient traditions blend with modernity.
With bustling cities and peaceful temples,
It's a place of beauty, history, and diversity.
From the neon lights of Tokyo,
To the serene gardens of Kyoto,
Japan captivates with its culture,
A land of samurais and geishas.
The cuisine is a work of art,
Sushi, ramen, and tempura delights the senses.
The tea ceremonies and kabuki performances,
Are a glimpse into the soul of the country.
Do you love Japan? The land of the rising sun,
Where discipline and honor are deeply ingrained.
With Mount Fuji towering in the distance,
It's a place that will forever remain.
So come and explore this magical land,
Immerse yourself in its beauty and wonder.
Japan will capture your heart,
Leaving you longing for more of its splendor.

103

Land of the Rising Sun

In the land of the rising sun, where food is love,
A culinary journey like no other,
Savoring the flavors, each dish a delicacy,
From sushi to tempura, each bite a treasure.

The dedication to perfection, a true art,
Respect for the ingredients, a sacred bond,
From the tender wagyu beef to the fresh seafood,
Every meal a celebration of the land.

The chefs, masters of their craft, create magic,
A symphony of flavors, a feast for the senses,
Eating here is not just sustenance,
But a deep appreciation for the land and its bounty.

So let us raise our chopsticks in gratitude,
For the love of food and the land of the rising sun,
Where every meal is a work of art,
And every bite a taste of pure bliss.

104

Love Letter from Japan

In the stillness of the night, a letter came,
From lands afar, where cherry blossoms bloom,
Inscribed with words that kindled love's soft flame,
A tender message from across the gloom.

Oh, Japan, your beauty knows no bounds,
Your culture rich, your spirit pure and true,
In every line, a grace that astounds,
A love so deep, it shines like morning dew.

To hold your words is like a sacred gift,
A bond that spans across the ocean's vast,
In whispered sighs, our hearts together drift,
With every beat, a love that's meant to last.

So let this letter be a gentle guide,
To lead us closer, side by side, in stride,
In love's embrace, forever we'll abide.

WABI-SABI 8

A little History of

W a b i - S a b i

To really understand **wabi** and **sabi** requires time and exposure to how they are used in action, kind of absorbing all the connotations as you read haiku that employs it. But these definitions are a good starting point:

wabi — cultivated simplicity and poverty, an austere sense of beauty—the beauty that comes from the simplicity of life, life in beautiful harmony with nature and minus materiality

sabi — patina, beauty through the marks of age, the celebration of that which is old and faded (but glorious in a sense), nostalgia; the idea that objects become more valuable and beautiful as they acquire "character" marks from use and wear and tear over the passage of time; it also incorporates an appreciation of the cycles of life, such as spring into autumn.

"In wabi-sabi, we find beauty in the perfectly imperfect."

105

Wabi-Sabi

In the simple things, the beauty lies,
Wabi-sabi, imperfect perfection seen with new eyes.
Cracked pottery, weathered wood, a symbol
Of life's impermanence, embraced as noble.

The rusted metal, the faded cloth,
Each mark telling a story, reminding us both
Of the passing of time, the fleeting moment
That we must cherish, for it is potent.

To find beauty in the flawed and old,
To see the value in what others may scold,
This is the essence of wabi-sabi,
A philosophy that teaches us to be happy.

For in our imperfections, we find grace,
A acceptance of ourselves in every case.
To embrace the imperfect, the worn, the weathered,
Is to find true beauty, forever treasured.

106

Worn and Withered

Imperfect beauty
Worn and weathered, still cherished
Wabi-sabi grace

Carefree

Amidst chaos, peace
Wabi-sabi in the fray
Carefree simplicity

Peace

Soft autumn whispers
Embracing imperfections
Peace found in decay

107

Beauty in the Imperfect

Embrace the flawed lines

Beauty found in imperfection

Perfectly imperfect

Wrinkled Hands

Wrinkled hands that hold

Memories of days long past

Love in fading light.

Love for the Elderly

Elderly hearts beat,

In love's enduring embrace,

Timeless bond unites.

108

Transience

Transient as the shadows cast by the setting sun,

Life's fleeting moments slip through our fingers,

Like grains of sand slipping through an hourglass.

We hold on tight, but time waits for no one.

The beauty of a blooming flower,

The laughter of a child at play,

These precious moments are but passing,

Gone in the blink of an eye.

We try to hold on to the memories,

To capture them in our hearts forever,

But they slip away, like water through a sieve,

Leaving only echoes of what once was.

And so we must embrace the transience,

For it is what gives life its poignancy,

Its richness, its depth,

And reminds us of the fragility of existence.

109

Natural Beauty

In the heart of nature's untouched grace,
There lies a beauty, serene and pure,
A beauty that with time can never fade,
For it is a beauty that will endure.
Her eyes like pools of crystal clear water,
Reflecting the world in its vibrant hues,
Her smile a beacon of warmth and laughter,
A gentle breeze that softly woos.
Her skin like petals of a blooming rose,
Soft and delicate to the touch,
Her hair a cascade of silken flows,
A crown of beauty that's oh so much.
In her, the earth's beauty is found,
A reflection of its wonders untold,
She is a vision of grace unbound,
A masterpiece of nature, a sight to behold.
Her natural beauty shines from within,
A light that brightens even the darkest night,
In her presence, the world seems to spin,
And all is bathed in a radiant light.

110

Impermanence

In the grand scheme of life, all things must change,
From mountains high to rivers flowing free.
The seasons shift, the weather rearrange,
Impermanence is the only guarantee.

The mighty oak that stands for centuries,
Will one day fall and return to the earth.
The bustling city with its energies,
Will crumble and decay for all its worth.

We strive to hold on tight to what we know,
But time will not be paused, it marches on.
Embrace the ever-changing ebb and flow,
For nothing under heaven stays for long.

So let us cherish each fleeting moment,
And find beauty in the passing of time.
For in impermanence, there lies a hint,
That life is but a fleeting, precious rhyme.

III

Imperfections

In life, humility reigns supreme,
A quality often overlooked,
Yet in its presence, greatness is seen,
A trait with which all must be hooked.

Asymmetry guides the world's design,
Imperfect shapes, unmatched lines,
Yet beauty in this chaos aligns,
Perfection fades, imperfections shine.

For in flaws we find individuality,
A uniqueness that sets us apart,
Embracing asymmetry with humility,
We reveal the beauty of the heart.

So let us not strive for perfect ways,
But revel in our flaws, our quirks,
For in humility and asymmetry,
Imperfection is where true beauty lurks.

112

Uketamo

In the quiet whispers of dusk, a soft melody,
Echoes through the air, floats like a feather.
Uketamo, the gentle strumming of strings,
A symphony of peace, a lullaby for the soul.

Each note a caress, soothing and pure,
A cascade of music, a river of harmony.
In its rhythm, we find solace, we find calm,
The world fades away, just the music remains.

The artist's hands dance, a masterful grace,
Crafting beauty from silence, from emptiness.
Uketamo, a spell woven with strings,
A gift of serenity, a treasure to cherish.

As night falls, the melody lingers,
A soft hum in the darkness, a guiding light.
Uketamo, a comfort in the chaos,
A reminder of the beauty in simplicity.

113

Be Excellent not Perfect

Strive for excellence, not perfection, in all you do,
For perfection is an unattainable goal,
But excellence is within your reach, it's true.
With effort and determination, you'll control

The outcome of your efforts, striving for the best,
Yet understanding that mistakes will be made.
It's in these moments we truly are put to the test,
Learning from our errors, not letting them fade.

Embrace the journey, the ups and the downs,
For it's in the process that growth will occur.
Don't be afraid to stumble, and don't frown,
Just pick yourself up and continue to endure.

In the pursuit of excellence, you will find success,
A fulfillment that perfection cannot bestow.
So strive for greatness, and you will impress
Not only others, but yourself, as you grow.

114

Life's Simplicity

The joy of life is in its simplicity,
In moments of pure clarity and ease.
Not in the chaos or the grand events,
But in the quiet peace that nature sends.

A simple walk among the trees,
The rustling leaves and gentle breeze.
A smile shared between good friends,
A love that never seems to end.

No need for riches or for fame,
Just grateful for each day that came.
The beauty found in little things,
In the melody that a song brings.

So let us cherish each moment,
And not take for granted this life we've been lent.
For the joy of life is in its simplicity,
In the love and laughter that sets us free.

115

Be Content with Life

Be content at where you are right now,
Amidst the chaos and the strife,
Find peace within, make a solemn vow,
To cherish every moment of your life.

For time is fleeting, never to return,
Embrace the present, let go of regret,
In every trial, a lesson you will learn,
A chance to grow, to evolve, to reset.

Don't dwell on what you lack or what could be,
But rather savor all that you possess,
In gratitude, find true serenity,
And in simplicity, find happiness.

So be content at where you are right now,
For in this moment, you have all you need,
Embrace the journey, let your heart allow,
And find fulfillment in every little deed.

116

Accept Your Imperfections

In the mirror I gaze upon my face,
Imperfect features staring back at me,
Tiny flaws scattered like stars in the sky,
Yet beauty found in each flaw I see.

A crooked smile, a scar upon my cheek,
Imperfect skin, not smooth and porcelain,
But in these flaws, I find a kind of grace,
A uniqueness that sets me apart.

For perfection lies not in flawless skin,
But in the acceptance of imperfection,
In embracing the flaws that make us whole,
And finding beauty in the flawed reflection.

So I will not shy away from my flaws,
But embrace them as a part of who I am,
For in imperfection, true beauty lies,
And in flaws, I find my strength and my charm.

MEMOIRS 9

117

Memoirs of Japan

In ancient lands of cherry blossoms fair,

Where legends dance through misty mountain air,

The memoirs of Japan tell tales untold,

Of warriors brave and hearts that turn to gold.

The gentle touch of nature's guiding hand,

A tranquil peace across the sacred land,

In temples old, where wisdom's whispers flow,

A harmony of past and present know.

Through paper walls, the secrets are revealed,

The delicate art of swords and stones concealed,

Each brush stroke tells a story of the past,

A heritage preserved, traditions last.

In silent gardens, spirits linger near,

The echoes of a thousand years we hear,

The memoirs of Japan, a timeless rhyme,

A legacy of grace, eternal prime.

118

Memories are all I have...

In the land of cherry blossoms and quiet streets,
Memories of Japan linger sweet,
Temples and tea ceremonies,
Cultural treasures found in every corner.

Lost in the maze of ancient traditions,
Geishas and samurais dance with precision,
Paper lanterns light up the night,
Whispers of a rich history take flight.

From bustling Tokyo to serene Kyoto,
Mountains and rivers in harmony flow,
Sushi and sake, a taste of Japan,
A world of wonder in this foreign land.

In the stillness of a bamboo forest,
In the beauty of a garden at rest,
Japanese memories weave a tapestry,
Of moments cherished eternally.

119

When we first met...

When we first met, it was an online dream,

A chance encounter in a digital realm,

Two souls unbeknownst, brought together by fate,

Through pixels and screens, love began to take shape.

Your words were a melody, sweet and sincere,

Creating a bond that was crystal clear,

Though miles apart, our hearts were entwined,

In cyberspace, a love so divine.

We shared our thoughts, our hopes, our fears,

Building a connection that spanned the years,

Through messages and calls, we grew closer still,

A love blossoming against all will.

And when finally we met in flesh and bone,

The love we felt had already grown,

No longer just words on a computer screen,

But a love that was real, pure and serene.

So here we stand, hand in hand,

Our love stronger than we ever planned,

For when we first met, it was an online dream,

But now, it's a reality, more than it seems.

120

Take what you can get...

Take what you can get, the world's not fair or just,
Opportunities come few and far between,
So seize each moment, grasp it with both hands,
For life is fleeting, time slips through our fingers.

Do not wait for perfect chances to arise,
But make the most of what is given to you,
For every small success, no matter how slight,
Can pave the way for greater things to come.

Take what you can get, be grateful for it all,
For even the smallest victories matter,
And in the end, it's not the grandiose wins,
But the humble triumphs that define our lives.

So do not be discouraged by setbacks,
Or compare your journey to others around,
Just keep moving forward, one step at a time,
And take what you can get, with a grateful heart.

121

Can we still be as one...

Can we still be as one, despite the distance

That separates us, miles apart from each other?

Can our love endure the trials and resistance

Of time and space, of burdens we discover?

The longing in my heart for your presence

Grows stronger with each passing day,

But I hold onto hope and patience

That we'll find a way to overcome and stay.

Though obstacles may come and go,

I believe in the power of our bond,

To weather the storms that blow,

And emerge stronger, together, and fond.

So let's hold onto the love we share,

And trust in the strength of our connection,

For with faith and perseverance, we'll dare

To defy the odds and find our resurrection.

Can we still be as one? The answer is yes,

For true love knows no boundaries,

And with unwavering faith and tenderness,

We'll always find a way to come together, as one entity.

122

To be together again

I wish for us to be together again,
To feel the warmth of your hand in mine,
To see the twinkle in your eyes,
And hear your laughter fill the air.

I miss the way we used to talk,
Sharing secrets and dreams,
And planning for the future,
Our hearts beating as one.

I long to walk beside you,
Through fields of green and skies of blue,
To feel the rhythm of our steps,
In perfect harmony.

I wish for us to be together again,
To make new memories and cherish the old,
To love each other with all our hearts,
And never let go.

123

Kimono

In folds of silk, the kimono's grace reveals,
A garment rich in history and lore,
Wrapping the body in colors bold and bright,
A symbol of tradition and elegance.

From intricate patterns to simple designs,
It tells a story of ancient Japan,
A culture steeped in beauty and tradition,
A garment meant to honor and adorn.

Each stitch handcrafted with precision and care,
A work of art that stands the test of time,
A piece of fabric that holds memories dear,
A symbol of grace and beauty defined.

In wearing the kimono, we pay homage,
To those who came before us, their legacy,
Their artistry forever preserved in threads,
A garment timeless, forever unfurled.

124

Yukata

In delicate folds of silk, the yukata drapes
Soft hues of summer, a whisper of the past
A garment of tradition, a timeless grace
Worn with pride, a symbol of culture's depth

Flowing sleeves, gentle on the skin they touch
A dance of movement, a painter's brushstroke
Embracing simplicity, in every thread sewn
A celebration of beauty, in its simplest form

From festive festivals to quiet evenings at home
The yukata adorns, a piece of history told
With every stitch, a story untold
In its elegant simplicity, a masterpiece unfolds.

125

Kamishimo

In ancient Japan, the samurai's attire,
A symbol of honor and tradition held dear.
The kamishimo, a garment of beauty,
Worn with pride by warriors as they prepare for battle.

The hakama, flowing pants of black and white,
Gathered at the waist, a mark of strength and grace.
The kataginu, a sleeveless jacket adorned,
With intricate patterns, a warrior's armor in cloth.

With every stitch, a story is told,
Of bravery and loyalty, of battles fought and won.
The kamishimo, a symbol of the samurai's code,
Of honor, respect, and duty above all else.

So let us remember the legacy they left,
In the folds of the kamishimo, their spirit lives on.
A tribute to the samurai, forever revered,
In the timeless beauty of their traditional attire.

126

Tea Ceremony

In a room filled with quiet reverence,
Tea leaves gently unfurl in steaming water,
Ceramic cups waiting to be filled with warmth.

The host moves with grace, each movement deliberate,
Pouring liquid amber into delicate vessels,
A ritual as ancient as time itself.

Guests sit in silence, savoring each sip,
The bitter and sweet mingling on their tongues,
A moment of stillness in a chaotic world.

Each cup tells a story, a journey from leaf to lip,
A tradition passed down through generations,
A reminder of our connection to nature.

As the last drops are savored,
The ceremony comes to an end,
Leaving in its wake a sense of peace and contentment.

127

It's okay to do so...

In Japan, it's perfectly fine to slurp,

Noodles twirling on chopsticks, a little burp,

No need to be polite, just enjoy the taste,

Savoring each bite with no need for haste.

The sound of slurping fills the air,

A sign of appreciation, a gesture so fair,

Noodles made with care, served hot and steaming,

In Japan, etiquette is just a way of dreaming.

So don't be shy, embrace the noise,

It's all part of the culinary joys,

Slurp away without a worry in sight,

In Japan, it's perfectly alright.

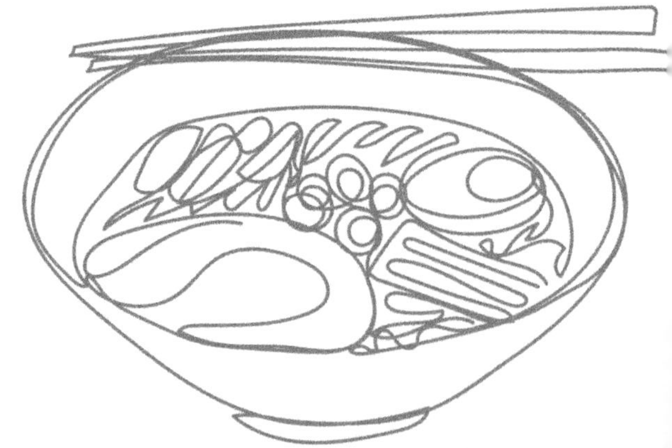

128

The Hakone Open-Air Museum

In Hakone's breeze, art comes alive,

Open-air museum, a haven for creativity.

Sculptures and installations, a visual feast,

Each piece telling a story, stirring emotions.

Amidst lush greenery and mountain views,

Visitors wander, immersed in beauty.

Bronze figures stand tall, frozen in time,

Capturing moments, invoking contemplation.

Children play, laughter fills the air,

As they explore and discover anew.

Past meets present, history preserved,

In this outdoor gallery, where art thrives.

A sanctuary of peace, a place of inspiration,

The Hakone Open-Air Museum, a true treasure.

Where whispers of the past echo through time,

And creativity knows no bounds.

129

teamLab Planets TOKYO

teamLab Planets TOKYO, a world of wonder

Where art and technology unite in harmony

Glowing orbs dance in a mesmerizing display

Reflecting our connection to nature's beauty

Fluid colors shift and swirl around us

Creating a dreamscape, a surreal landscape

We lose ourselves in this immersive realm

Where reality blurs and imagination takes flight

Each step we take, each turn we make

Reveals a new realm of possibility

A sensory overload, a visual symphony

That captivates and enthralls our senses

teamLab Planets TOKYO, a sanctuary of art

Where creativity knows no bounds

We are transported to a world unknown

And emerge transformed, our spirits lifted high

130

Tokyo National Museum

In the heart of Tokyo stands a grand museum,
Home to treasures of ancient days gone by.
Houses of history, art, and culture bloom,
In Tokyo National Museum, they lie.

Silent guardians of Japan's past reside,
Samurai armor gleaming in the light.
Porcelain plates from centuries beside,
Whispers of elegance, fragile and bright.

Paintings tell stories of a bygone age,
Cherry blossoms bloom in delicate hue.
Craftsmanship preserved on each written page,
In Tokyo National Museum so true.

Through the halls, echoes of the past ring clear,
A nation's heritage held dear and near.

131

Ghibli Museum Mitaka

In Mitaka, a haven for Ghibli fans,

A museum stands with whimsy and delight.

Where Totoro greets with his endearing grin,

And Catbus waits to whisk you out of sight.

Inside, a world of magic comes alive,

Through films and art that captivate the soul.

Each frame a masterpiece, a treasure trove,

Of wonder, joy, and tales that make us whole.

The garden whispers secrets of the past,

As robots roam and creatures dance with glee.

A place where dreams and reality collide,

In Ghibli's realm, where hearts are wild and free.

So come and wander through this wondrous place,

Where creativity and love abound.

In Mitaka's museum, dreams take flight,

And Ghibli's spirit forever can be found.

132

Nezu Museum

Upon the hill, the Nezu Museum stands tall,
A haven for art, beauty, and tranquility.
Its gardens bloom with careful design,
A peaceful refuge amidst the bustling city.

Within its walls, treasures await to behold,
Ancient artifacts from a distant past.
Each piece tells a story, whispers of history,
A glimpse into Japan's rich cultural tapestry.

The quiet halls echo with the footsteps of visitors,
Murmurs of admiration and wonder.
Here, time slows down, a moment of reflection,
As we immerse ourselves in the art's perfection.

The Nezu Museum, a sanctuary of art and nature,
A place of serenity, a sanctuary for the soul.
In its presence, we find peace and inspiration,
A timeless beauty that will forever endure.

These last couple of poems are of great museums in Japan. If you love art,
these places are for you.

FOR HIM 10

133

For Him...

For him, I write these words of love and grace,
My heart overflowing with pure devotion.
His smile, a beacon in life's darkest maze,
Guiding me through love's endless ocean.

With each passing day, my love only grows,
Stronger, deeper, an unbreakable bond.
In his arms, all my worries and woes,
Fade away, in his love, I am found.

I cherish every moment we share,
Every laugh, every smile, every tear.
For him, I would move mountains, I swear,
For his love, I would face any fear.

He is my rock, my light, my everything,
In his arms, I find solace and peace.
For him, my heart will forever sing,
A song of love that will never cease.

134

From a Secret Admirer

From a secret admirer, to you my love,
I've watched from afar, like a dove,
My heart beats fast, my thoughts a whirl,
My feelings for you, like a precious pearl.

I've admired you in silence, for far too long,
But now I must confess, in this sweet song,
You're the one I dream of, day and night,
In your presence, everything feels just right.

Your smile lights up my darkest days,
Your laughter is like a beautiful blaze,
I long to hold you close, to feel your touch,
To love you deeply, oh, how much.

I send you this message, from my heart to yours,
Hoping you'll see, what my love ensures,
I may be just a secret admirer for now,
But in time, I hope to make you mine somehow.

135

He doesn't know...

He walks by, his eyes fixed on the distance,
Unaware of my presence, my existence.
I watch from afar, my heart aching with longing,
But to him, I am simply a face in the throng.

I yearn to speak, to catch his attention,
To show him the depth of my affection.
But silence holds me in its icy grip,
And my love for him remains unspoken, a secret trip.

He doesn't know I exist, in his world so bright,
I am but a shadow, a flicker of light.
Yet in my heart, he reigns supreme,
A king of my dreams, a fantasy extreme.

I will keep my love hidden, a silent flame,
And cherish the moments he doesn't know my name.
For in my mind, he's all that I need,
Even if he doesn't know I exist, my heart will still bleed.

136

I love him from afar...

I love him from afar, a secret flame
That burns within my soul, unseen by all
I watch him from a distance, longing eyes
Aching with the knowledge of my unspoken love

I dare not speak it, for fear of rejection
Of losing what little I have of him
So I keep my feelings hidden, buried deep
And admire him silently, from afar

I cherish every moment, every glance
Treasure every word, every smile
I hold onto these fleeting memories
And dream of a love that may never be

Yet still, I love him, in my own quiet way
Content to bask in the warmth of his presence
To be near him, even if only in spirit
For my love knows no bounds, even from afar.

137

I admire him...

I admire him, his strength and steady gaze,

In times of doubt, he stands there unafraid.

His actions speak when words may fall astray,

A pillar of support in every way.

Through trials and tribulations, he remains,

A beacon in the storm, a steady flame.

His kindness knows no bounds, his heart so pure,

In every action, love and grace endure.

I watch in awe as he navigates

The challenges of life with such grace.

His wisdom guides him through each twist and turn,

I am in awe of all that I have learned.

I admire him, his courage and his heart,

His gentle spirit, a work of art.

In every moment, I am inspired,

By the man I admire, so admired.

138

Does he feel the same...

What are your feelings towards me, I wonder

Do you see me as a fleeting thought, or something more

Do you feel a spark when we're together, or is it all in my head

I long to know the truth, to understand what lies in your heart

My nights are filled with dreams of you

Thoughts of your smile, your laugh, your touch

I find myself lost in a sea of uncertainty

Hoping that you feel the same way I do

But words remain unspoken, feelings kept hidden

I fear rejection, the thought of losing you

Yet I cannot keep these emotions bottled up inside

I must know, I must hear the truth from your lips

So tell me, what are your feelings towards me

Do you see a future with us, or are we just passing ships

I long for clarity, for honesty, for a chance to be with you

Until then, I'll hold onto hope, and wait for your answer.

139

What's in our future?

Do we have a future together, my love?

A question that fills my heart with doubt.

Will our paths continue to intertwine,

Or will they diverge, leading us apart?

I long to gaze into your eyes and know

That we will grow old side by side,

Facing life's challenges hand in hand,

Our love as strong as the ocean tide.

But uncertainty lingers in the air,

A whisper of fear that creeps in.

Will our love withstand the tests of time,

Or will it crumble, fragile as sand?

I want to believe that we are meant to be,

That our souls are bound together,

But the future remains a mystery,

An unwritten chapter waiting to unfold.

So let us cherish each moment we have,

And hold on to the love we share.

For in this fleeting, fragile world,

Our bond is a treasure beyond compare.

140

My deep desire...

I have a deep desire for him, so strong,
His presence fills my heart with pure delight,
In his arms, I know I truly belong,
Each moment spent with him feels just right.

His laughter lights up every darkened space,
His smile, a beacon in the night,
I could gaze upon his handsome face
For hours, and never tire of the sight.

His voice, a melody that soothes my soul,
His touch, a warmth that sets me ablaze,
In his embrace, I feel completely whole,
Lost in the beauty of his loving gaze.

I have a deep desire for him, pure and true,
My heart belongs to him, forever and anew.

141

Japanese Man

My Japanese man so wise and gentle,
With eyes that hold ancient wisdom.
His laughter floats like cherry blossoms,
And his touch is as light as a feather.

In his presence, I find peace
And a sense of belonging.
He moves with grace and poise,
A true embodiment of harmony.

He speaks in soft melodies,
His words a song of love and devotion.
I am captivated by his culture,
And I am honored to learn from him.

My Japanese man, a treasure
Whose heart is pure and true.
I am grateful for his presence,
For in him, I have found a piece of heaven.

142

Powerful

He's so powerful, a force to be reckoned with,

His presence commands attention, admiration,

With every step he takes, a trail of awe,

A lion among sheep, a leader in his domain.

His voice resonates with authority and strength,

His gaze pierces through the souls of men,

He holds the power to inspire, to uplift,

To shape the world around him and within.

In his hands, the world is but a plaything,

He molds it to his will, bends it to his design,

Yet with such power comes a heavy burden,

The weight of expectation, of consequence.

He knows the price of power, the sacrifices made,

The loneliness that comes with being at the top,

But still he stands tall, unyielding, unafraid,

For he knows that true power lies in how it's used.

He's so powerful, a force of nature,

A titan among mortals, a beacon of light,

And though he may falter, stumble, fall,

He will rise again, stronger than before.

143

Do you know me...

Do you even know me, my love
Or am I but a stranger in your eyes
A fleeting shadow passing by
In the vast expanse of your mind.

Do you know the thoughts that plague me
The fears that keep me up at night
Do you see the tears that fall
When I am alone in the darkness.

Do you know the dreams I hold
The hopes that keep me moving forward
Do you understand the depths of my soul
The complexities that make me who I am.

Do you know me, truly know me
Or are we just two ships passing in the night
Bound by love but separated by distance
I long for you to see me, to know me.

144

Undying Love

In the garden of forever blooms a love,
An undying flame that burns eternal bright.
Through storm and drought, it stands strong and true,
A beacon in the darkest, loneliest night.

No force of nature, no passing of time
Can shake the bond that binds two hearts as one.
Through joy and sorrow, hand in hand they climb,
A tale of love that's never truly done.

Like petals on a flower, their love unfolds,
With each new day a chapter to be told.
Through trials and triumphs, highs and lows,
Their love endures, unbroken and bold.

So let us cherish this precious gift,
This undying love that makes our spirits lift.
For in a world so full of pain and strife,
Love is the one true constant in this life.

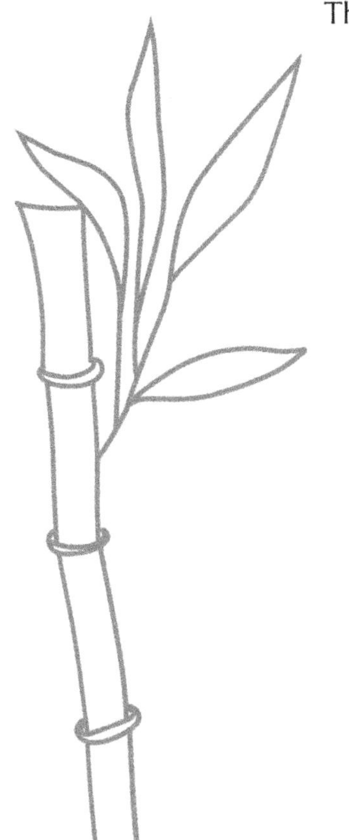

145

My first letter from him...

A single sheet of paper, inked with words so sweet
A letter from the one I adore, my heart skips a beat
His words flow like a gentle stream, soothing my soul
Each line filled with love, making me whole

In his handwriting, I see his tender touch
His thoughts, his feelings, expressed so much
I read and reread his words, feeling his presence near
His love for me, crystal clear

I hold the letter close, its warmth enveloping me
His love shining through, setting my spirit free
I treasure this letter, a precious gift from him
A love letter to cherish, my heart brimming to the brim

With each word he writes, he captures my heart
In his letter, I find solace, never to part
My first letter from him, a token of his love
A treasure to hold onto, sent from above.

146

I meant every word...

I meant every word I ever said to him,
Each declaration, each promise kept true.
My love for him, endless and unswerving,
My heart whispers in the quiet of night.

I promised him forever, a love that lasts,
Through trials and triumphs, through joy and sorrow.
I meant it all, every word sincere,
My love for him, unwavering and pure.

I spoke of dreams and hopes we'd share,
Of adventures yet to come, of memories made.
I meant every word, written in the stars,
A love that transcends time and space.

I meant it all, every promise made,
My heart beats for him, my soul intertwined.
I meant every word, spoken with love,
For he is my everything, my forevermore.

147

Let's meet my love...

We will meet, and when we do, time will stand still,

Our eyes will lock, our hearts will start to fill

With emotions too powerful to contain,

A connection so strong, it's hard to explain.

Our souls will dance in perfect harmony,

In that moment, we'll be wild and free.

The world around us will fade away,

Leaving just us in our own little play.

We'll laugh and talk for hours on end,

Our friendship growing with every bend.

We'll share our dreams and fears alike,

Knowing in each other we've found our light.

So let us meet, and when we do,

Let's cherish this bond so pure and true.

For in each other, we've found a treasure,

A friendship that will last forever.

MT. FUJI 11

148

Mt. Fuji

Behold majestic Mt. Fuji, grand and tall,
Its snow-capped peak reaching towards the sky,
A symbol of Japan, revered by all,
Its beauty and grace, none can deny.

Silent sentinel, watching over lands,
Majestic in its stillness and its might,
A vision of serenity so grand,
Guiding travelers through day and night.

A sacred place for those who seek to find
Peace and solace in its quiet embrace,
Where spirits soar and hearts are aligned,
In harmony with nature's whispered grace.

Oh Mt. Fuji, ancient and revered,
Your presence brings a sense of calm and peace,
A timeless beauty that will never fade,
A symbol of Japan that will never cease.

149

Honshu

Honshu, land of ancient temples and bustling cities,
Where cherry blossoms bloom in spring's gentle breeze.
From Tokyo's neon lights to Kyoto's historic streets,
This island holds secrets of old and new to meet.

Mount Fuji stands tall, a majestic sight to behold,
Its snow-capped peak glistening in the sun's golden fold.
Rice fields stretch out, mirroring the sky above,
A landscape of beauty and tranquility, full of love.

In Hiroshima, a somber reminder of war's tragic past,
Yet a symbol of hope and peace that will forever last.
The people of Honshu carry on with grace and pride,
Their culture and traditions, a timeless guide.

So let us journey to Honshu, where the heart of Japan lies,
A land of wonder and mystery under endless skies.
From the mountains to the sea, in every corner and crease,
Honshu beckons us to explore, to find inner peace.

150

Three Holy Mountains

In Japan, three mountains stand tall and proud,

Among the holiest, shrouded in clouds.

Fuji, the most famous, majestic and grand,

A symbol of strength across the land.

Tateyama, with its snow-capped peak,

A place for pilgrims to seek and seek.

And Haku-san, pure as the driven snow,

Where prayers of reverence softly flow.

Each mountain holds a sacred power,

A connection to nature in its finest hour.

Three holy mountains, revered and true,

In Japan, they stand, a spiritual view.

151

Mount Tate Japan

In Honshu's heart, Mount Tate stands tall and proud,
A testament to nature's strength and beauty.
Its snow-capped peaks reach for the clouds above,
A sight that takes my breath away each time.

The rugged terrain, a challenge to all who dare
To climb its slopes and brave its icy winds.
But those who do are rewarded with a view
That fills the soul with awe and gratitude.

The trees that clothe its base in greenery,
A stark contrast to the barren rocks above.
The silence of the mountain's ancient slopes,
A reminder of the power of the earth.

As I stand in awe at Mount Tate's feet,
I am humbled by its majesty and grace.
A sacred place where nature reigns supreme,
And humanity is but a fleeting guest.

152

Mount Haku Japan

Mount Haku stands tall, majestic and serene,

A towering peak in Japan, so pristine.

Its snowy crown glistens in the sun's soft light,

A beacon of beauty, a breathtaking sight.

The forests below whisper tales untold,

Of ancient wisdom and legends bold.

The mountain's silence speaks of time gone by,

A sacred place where the spirits fly.

In every season, its splendor is seen,

In blooming cherry blossoms, in winter's sheen.

A place of peace, of harmony and grace,

Mount Haku's beauty, no one can erase.

So let us cherish this mountain so grand,

An emblem of Japan, a symbol so grand.

Mount Haku, standing tall in all its glory,

A symbol of nature's eternal story.

Shizuoka

153

In Shizuoka, where mountains meet the sea,
Green tea fields stretch as far as eyes can see.
Mt. Fuji's silhouette looms in the distance,
A symbol of Japan's natural existence.

Sushi stalls bustling with laughter and cheer,
Sakura blossoms painting the streets so dear.
Ancient temples whisper secrets of old,
History and tradition beautifully unfold.

Onsen retreats offer relaxation divine,
Hot springs to soothe both body and mind.
The gentle waves of Suruga Bay greet the shore,
Calm and serene, forever wanting more.

In Shizuoka, beauty and harmony reign,
A place where nature and culture remain.
An enchanting escape from the world's haste,
Where peace and tranquility find a place.

154

Yamanashi

In fields of green and mountains capped with snow,
Yamanashi's beauty shows with grace and poise.
The Fuji-san looms in splendor, a sight to behold,
Its presence commands respect, a towering giant.

Vineyards stretch with rows of grapevines,
Their fruit ripening under the sun's embrace.
Winery tours beckon with promises of taste,
A sip of Yamanashi's finest, a moment of bliss.

Cherry blossoms scatter in the springtime breeze,
Painting the landscape with pink and white petals.
Hiking trails winding through forests thick,
Nature's symphony sings in harmony.

Hot springs bubble with rejuvenating heat,
A soak in mineral waters, a soothing retreat.
Yamanashi's allure, a treasure to behold,
A haven for the soul, a sanctuary of peace.

155

Let's Go Hiking

In Japan, the hiking trails wind through lush forests,

A tapestry of green, dotted with cherry blossoms,

Each step a journey into nature's embrace,

The sound of a babbling brook as a guide.

Mountains rise majestically in the distance,

Inviting us to explore their ancient peaks,

The scent of pine lingering in the air,

A symphony of birdsong as our soundtrack.

Through valleys and over wooden bridges we wander,

The path unfurling like a ribbon before us,

A sense of serenity washing over our souls,

As we disconnect from the modern world's chaos.

In Japan, the hiking trails are a sacred escape,

A chance to reconnect with the earth and with ourselves,

To find peace in the simplicity of nature's beauty,

And discover the magic that lies within.

156

Let's Pick Pine Nuts

Let's pick pine nuts in Japan, beneath the trees so tall,
Where autumn leaves are falling, in colors of the fall.
The air is crisp and clean, the sky a brilliant blue,
As we gather golden treasures, nature's gift to me and you.

The forest whispers secrets, in a language all its own,
As we wander through the pine grove, feeling fully grown.
The scent of cedar fills the air, a fragrance pure and sweet,
Guiding us along the path, our harvest to complete.

With nimble fingers, we pluck the nuts from cones of green,
Their earthy flavor beckoning, a taste yet to be seen.
We gather up our bounty, in baskets made of wicker,
Our hearts light and happy, our spirits growing quicker.

Let's pick pine nuts in Japan, a timeless act of grace,
Connecting us to nature, in this tranquil space.
For in this simple moment, we find peace and joy,
As we gather nature's treasures, like a child's favorite toy.

157

Escape to Fuji

Escape to Fuji, a dream we hold so tight,
Where mountains high reach up to touch the sky,
And cherry blossoms paint the scene so bright,
A peaceful pause from life's relentless cry.

The air is crisp, the silence pure and clear,
As we ascend the trails to find our peace,
In solitude, away from doubt and fear,
Our hearts are light, our burdens start to cease.

The beauty of this sacred land unfolds,
In shades of green and blue, a perfect blend,
A soothing balm for weary hearts consoled,
By nature's grace, on which we can depend.

So let us lose ourselves in Fuji's arms,
And find our solace in her quiet charms.

158

Paint the Sky Pink

In a frame, a vision of delicate blooms,
Cherry blossoms in soft hues of pink and white,
Captured in time, a moment frozen still,
Each petal whispers secrets in the light.

Branches reaching towards the azure sky,
Dancing in the gentle springtime breeze,
A symphony of beauty for the eye,
Nature's artistry, a gift to please.

Their fragility a fleeting grace,
Yet in their brevity, they hold such power,
A reminder of life's transient pace,
In every bloom, a moment to devour.

So let us pause and linger in this scene,
Amidst the blossoms' whispered reverie,
A painting of cherry blossoms serene,
A masterpiece of nature's harmony.

159

Painting of Mt. Fuji

In hues of blue and green, Mt. Fuji stands tall,
A symbol of Japan, revered by all.
Its snow-capped peak reaching towards the sky,
A sight that brings wonder to every eye.

Each stroke of the brush captures its grandeur,
The artist's skill making the scene all the purer.
Majestic and serene, it looms in the distance,
A timeless beauty, an eternal existence.

The painting of Mt. Fuji, a work of art,
Inspiring awe and reverence in every heart.
Its tranquil presence a calming force,
A reminder of nature's unyielding course.

As we gaze upon this masterpiece divine,
We feel a sense of peace, a moment sublime.
Mt. Fuji, forever immortalized in paint,
A symbol of beauty, never to faint.

Fuji-san

Majestic Fuji
Snow-capped peak in morning light
Eternal beauty

Beauty of Fuji

Giant Fuji stands tall
Snow-capped peak glowing brightly
Nature's beauty shines

Mountain Air

Mountain air so pure
Fuji stands tall and serene
Nature's peace endures

161

Japanese Proverb of Fuji

'A wise man climbs Mt Fuji once, only a fool climbs it twice."

162

Konohanasakuya-hime

In the realm of Mount Fuji, she reigns supreme,
Konohanasakuya-hime, goddess of flowers.
Her beauty rivals the blossoms in spring,
A symbol of grace and delicate power.

She walks among the cherry trees with ease,
Her presence brings life to the barren earth.
Her touch is gentle, her smile pure and sweet,
She embodies the beauty of rebirth.

Her spirit shines like the fiery sun,
A beacon of hope in a darkened world.
She is the protector of all that blooms,
A guardian of nature, her spirit unfurled.

So let us honor Konohanasakuya-hime,
In her grace and beauty, we find our own.
May her spirit guide us through the seasons of life,
And lead us to a world where love is sown.

GOODBYE JAPAN 12

163

Good-bye Japan

Sakura petals fall,

Whispers of farewell in wind,

Goodbye Japan's grace.

See you again!

Cherry blossoms bloom

Land of the rising sun calls

Japan, I will return

164

Japan, Adieu!

Land of the rising sun
Cherry blossoms softly fall
My heart bids farewell

Bloom and Die

Pink petals fall fast
Cherry blossoms bloom with grace
Brief beauty embraced

165

I left my heart in Tokyo

I left my heart in Tokyo,

Amidst the bustling city streets,

Where neon lights and ancient shrines meet,

A place where dreams and reality flow.

The cherry blossoms in full bloom,

Painted skies in shades of pink,

Whispers of the past in every link,

In this city, my heart found its room.

Lost in the crowds of Shibuya's maze,

Lost in translation, yet connected,

To a place where traditions are respected,

To a city where memories amaze.

I left my heart in Tokyo,

But it will always be mine to keep,

A piece of me in those streets so deep,

In this city, my love will forever flow.

166

Good-bye Totoro

Goodbye Totoro, with your fluffy belly and friendly face,
You brought us joy and laughter in this magical place.
Your whiskers twitched and eyes so bright,
You made our troubles take flight.

In the forest green, where spirits roam,
You made us feel safe, never alone.
Your gentle paws and wise old eyes,
Your kindness never a guise.

But now the time has come to say farewell,
As the seasons change and we must dwell.
In memories we'll keep you close,
Our friendship forever froze.

So goodbye Totoro, may your spirit soar,
In the winds of time, forevermore.
To the next adventure, we must go,
But in our hearts, you'll always glow.

167

Hello Kitty

In a world of pink and bows, she reigns supreme,
Hello Kitty, with her cute and innocent face,
Adored by young and old alike,
Bringing joy and smiles with each tiny pace.

Her whiskers twitch, her eyes bright with delight,
A symbol of friendship and love,
In a world that can sometimes feel dark,
She shines like a beacon from above.

With her friends by her side, she explores,
The wonders of a magical land,
Filled with laughter and endless fun,
Together, they always lend a helping hand.

So here's to Hello Kitty, our favorite feline,
Forever young and forever pure,
A reminder of the simple joys in life,
That we can always rely on to endure.

168

Study Japanese

Studying Japanese, a student's noble quest,
To master words and phrases of the East,
Kanji characters, intricate and complex,
Hiragana and Katakana, a challenge indeed.

With textbooks and flashcards in hand,
I pour over lessons, determined to understand,
The beauty of this ancient language,
A culture rich and history profound.

Through grammar drills and vocabulary tests,
I strive to improve, to do my best,
To speak with fluency and grace,
In every conversation, find my place.

Oh, the joy of learning a tongue so new,
Of exploring a world beyond what I knew,
Studying Japanese, a student's delight,
A journey of discovery, infinite.

169

Make new friends....

Make new friends, with open hearts we seek

To find connection, kindred spirits speak

In shared laughter, trust and joy we find

A bond that grows, in friendship we're entwined

We share our stories, hopes and dreams unfold

In each other's company, we find gold

New perspectives, wisdom to impart

In friendship's embrace, we open our heart

Together we explore, new paths we tread

With newfound friends, no longer led

Alone in solitude, we now stand tall

In friendship's embrace, we find our all

So let us reach out, to those unknown

For in their eyes, a kindred spirit shown

Make new friends, let love and kindness be

The bond that binds us, for eternity.

170

Don't forget, before you leave...

Before you leave, don't forget to pray

At a Japanese temple, where silence reigns.

The soft rustle of leaves in the breeze,

The scent of incense, floating on the air.

Breathe in deeply, let your worries fade

As you bow in reverence, a quiet nod

To the gods who watch over us all.

Find peace in the stillness of this sacred space.

Offer a prayer for those you love,

For yourself, for guidance on your path.

Feel the weight of your burdens lift

As you surrender to the divine.

Don't rush through this moment of reflection,

Let it linger, let it seep into your soul.

For in this sacred place, there is power

In the quietude, in the stillness of prayer.

And as you leave, lighter and more centered,

Carry with you the serenity you found.

Remember this moment, hold it close,

And know that you can always return.

171

To Japan, with Love,

Oh Japan, how I love thee with all my heart,
Your cherry blossoms blooming, a work of art.
From Mount Fuji's majestic peak so high,
To Kyoto's ancient temples standing by.

Your culture rich in tradition and grace,
Tea ceremonies and kimono's embrace.
Sumo wrestling and manga tales so bold,
Samurai history told and retold.

Sushi and ramen, a culinary delight,
Street vendors selling yakitori at night.
Onsen baths and geisha's elegant dance,
In every corner, a new romance.

Oh Japan, land of rising sun and sea,
Forever in my heart, you'll always be.
With reverence and respect, I'll forever shout,
Love you Japan, without a doubt!

172

Canada!

In the land of maple leaves and winter snow,
Canada, my heart belongs to thee,
From east to west, from sea to shining sea,
I've wandered far, but now I rest and grow.

The Rockies stand in all their grandeur high,
A testament to nature's awe-inspiring might,
And in the prairies, golden fields stretch out of sight,
The beauty of this land will never die.

From Toronto's bustling city streets,
To Vancouver's mountains touching sky,
In Montreal, where cultures blend and meet,
I find my soul at peace, no need to fly.

Canada, my true north strong and free,
In your embrace, I've found my home to be.

173

Now catch your flight!

Catch your flight, the time is drawing near,

The plane awaits, its engines start to hum,

The journey ahead, so full of promise and fear,

Leaving behind the familiar, into the unknown we come.

Boarding pass in hand, we make our way,

Through bustling crowds and security lines,

Anxious hearts beating, thoughts in disarray,

But excitement shines in our eyes like a beacon that shines.

The plane takes off, lifting us high,

Above the clouds, the world below a blur,

In this moment, we're free to fly,

To new adventures, to explore and to endure.

So spread your wings and soar up high,

Embrace the journey, embrace the flight,

For in this moment, under this vast sky,

We are alive, we are free, we are in flight.

OTHER BOOKS BY THE AUTHOR

POETRY
. Love Letter's From Japan
. Soul Food
. Love Stories from the Heart
(COMING SOON)

CHILDREN'S BOOKS
. Toshi and the missing Ball-y
. Toshi visits London, England
. Toshi visits Pairs, France
. Toshi in Tokyo
. Toshi and his human sisters

NOVELS
. The Kingdom of Arundel Series Books
. Samantha Cooper HATES Bullies
(COMING SOON)

A Note on the Author

Dina Ezzeddine is a writer and illustrator from
Canada. Dina has a degree in Visual Arts and Design,
as well as a Bachelor of Arts degree in English. Dina
has written numerous children's book and numerous
teen books. This book of poetry is her latest work.
You can find more of Dina's upcoming work online!

Find more of Dina's here:
visit Amazon & Barnes & Noble
e-books available everywhere.

---

author_illustratordina
aiko10195@gmail.com

Extract from upcoming book
Love Letters From Japan

In a land of cherry blossoms and tea,
Love letters from Japan arrive to me.
In elegant kanji characters they are penned,
Words of affection that never seem to end.

Each stroke of the brush, so delicate and fine,
Expresses love that's truly divine.
The paper whispers secrets from afar,
Carrying messages like a shining star.

With reverence, I unfold each one,
Savoring the beauty of the rising sun.
In every line, a piece of the sender's heart,
A connection that will never depart.

Though miles apart, our hearts still entwine,
Through love letters from Japan, so pure and kind.
A reminder that love transcends all space,
And brings us closer in this divine embrace.